College Aspirations and Access in Working-Class Rural Communities

Social Class in Education

Series Editors: Buffy Smith, St. Thomas University, and Victoria Svoboda, University of Wisconsin-La Crosse

While education is often heralded as a means to social mobility, educational outcomes suggest that schools, colleges, and universities actually replicate rather than transforming social class inequities. Social Class in Education focuses on the ways in which social and socioeconomic class issues, broadly defined, impact educational experiences and outcomes. We invite submissions from scholars focused on Pre-K through postsecondary environments, as well as manuscripts that explore intersections of classism and other forms of identities and oppressions. We aim to expand the conversation about how class is defined, measured, and experienced in educational settings. Scholars who use theoretical frameworks such as critical race theory, reproduction theory, and feminist theories are especially encouraged to submit proposals, though the series is open to other considerations. Successful proposals will be accessible to a multidisciplinary audience, and advance our understanding of social class, its impact on educational outcomes, and practical suggestions for narrowing economic inequality in school settings.

Recent Titles in This Series

College Aspirations and Access in Working-Class Rural Communities

The Mixed Signals, Challenges, and New Language First-Generation Students Encounter

Sonja Ardoin

LEXINGTON BOOKS
Lanham • Boulder • New York • London

Published by Lexington Books
An imprint of The Rowman & Littlefield Publishing Group, Inc.
4501 Forbes Boulevard, Suite 200, Lanham, Maryland 20706
www.rowman.com

Unit A, Whitacre Mews, 26-34 Stannary Street, London SE11 4AB

British Library Cataloguing in Publication Information Available

The hardback edition of this book was previously catalogued by the Library of Congress
as follows:

Library of Congress Cataloging-in-Publication Data

Names: Ardoin, Sonja, author.
Title: College aspirations and access in working-class rural communities :
   the mixed signals, challenges, and new language first-generation students
   encounter / Sonja Ardoin.
Description: Lanham : Lexington Books, [2017] | Series: Social class in
   education | Includes bibliographical references and index.
Identifiers: LCCN 2017054023 (print) | LCCN 2017044049 (ebook) | ISBN
   9781498536875 (electronic) | ISBN 9781498536868 (cloth : alk. paper)
Subjects: LCSH: Working class—Education (Higher)—United States. |
   First-generation college students—United States. | Student
   aspirations—United States. | Academic language--Study and
   teaching—United States.
Classification: LCC LC5051 (print) | LCC LC5051 .A76 2017 (ebook) | DDC
   379.2/6—dc23
LC record available at https://lccn.loc.gov/2017054023

ISBN 978-1-4985-3686-8 (cloth : alk. paper)
ISBN 978-1-4985-3688-2 (pbk. : alk. paper)
ISBN 978-1-4985-3687-5 (electronic)

♾ ™ The paper used in this publication meets the minimum requirements of American
National Standard for Information Sciences—Permanence of Paper for Printed Library
Materials, ANSI/NISO Z39.48-1992.

Printed in the United States of America

To all the students from MapDots:
snub statistics and supposed-tos; you can *do whatever*
you want and be whoever you want!
you possess many talents and have much to contribute.
know that. believe it. show the world.

To all the folks who support those students and their journeys:
you are appreciated and valued and loved.
we are grateful and indebted.

And to my own MapDot:
I could not imagine calling any other place or people home.
home is what you will always be to me.
I claim you proudly.

Contents

Foreword

Growing up in central North Dakota offered big open skies, vast landscapes, and friendly people. It also presented many challenges for understanding the world of college. Sharing my experiences of growing up in a rural area often shocks and sometimes amuses colleagues. This is both surprising and disappointing to me as very well-intentioned and educated individuals know little about the vast population of nearly 50 million people who live in rural areas in the United States.

When I share with colleagues that I graduated with eight other individuals in my senior class, most are stunned. My public school included kindergarten through twelfth grade and enrolled 112 students. It was closed in 1992 having an enrollment of just over 50 students. This is just one ramification of the continuously declining population of the town, which today has approximately 100 residents.

Growing up in a rural environment is alien to so many, yet it is all that others know. To complicate matters, rural can look different for each person living in a small town and for each person living on a farm many miles from a small town. Rural environments are often discussed as less than suburban or urban areas, when in fact, they are just different.

Rural students are complex in the multiple identities they hold; many rural students are also first-generation college students and some have poor or working-class backgrounds. Our geographic origin is often associated with our race, social class, culture, and other identities. Thus, talking about rural students is complicated. We know much more about the successes and challenges of low-income students, first-generation students, and students of color. Yet, these students can also be rural students, which adds a unique dimension to their identity that affects who they are, what they think and know about college, how they finance college, what majors they seek, and so much more.

Dr. Ardoin's book, *College Aspirations and Access in Working-Class, Rural Communities: The Mixed Signals, Challenges, and New Language First-Generation Students Encounter,* offers us an opportunity to reflect on the experiences of rural students and those that support rural students. She shares both the advantages and disadvantages of growing up rural. Despite the large rural population in the United States, rural students are largely invisible to policymakers and educators. Dr. Ardoin explores how rural, working-class, first-generation college students understand the college process, and her findings suggest how educators and policymakers can better support rural students in their pursuit of higher education.

Rural for me meant that there was no guidance counselor in my school, no school official discussing the college experience. College or university staff did not visit my school, nor did students attend college visits. My guidance counselor was my brother. I was fortunate to have older siblings that had attended college, and my brother served as my guide. He told me what college to attend and what major to choose. I did not know I could attend a school out of state and was only vaguely familiar with the idea that there were other colleges out of state. I did not know the different institutional types. I was not aware that there were colleges serving only women or that focused on a liberal arts education. In fact, I did not know what liberal arts was all together. I was not aware the costs of college. I did know that I was likely going to pay for college by selling my cattle. I knew that my mother had always wanted to go to college and was adamant that I attend college, but I did not know why. I did what others told me in relation to college and never questioned their college knowledge. Dr. Ardoin discusses the complexity of understanding the college process and how many rural students are disadvantaged by their lack of college knowledge and the lack of college-going culture in their schools and communities.

I applied to the one college my brother suggested, and I noted on my application the major my brother told me to seek. On my application I wrote, "business administration." It turns out there was no major in business administration at this institution as students would need to choose a major within business such as finance, marketing, or accounting. I was placed into public administration instead. My lack of college knowledge continued even after enrolling. My first academic advisor told me I was not in business administration and should continue with public administration as it afforded me many options, and I said, "Ok," just as I said to my brother when he advised me on all other college decisions. In this book, Dr. Ardoin explores what it means to live in a rural area without access to information or informed individuals who can guide and support students in the college process.

Rural students are often invisible as they fit no particular demographic, yet many have multiple underrepresented identities. Particularly in today's environment, educated individuals make assumptions about the lack of knowledge and understanding that rural students possess. Rural students are typecast as not being smart, having "backward" or limited perspectives about local, national, or global issues, or having no interest in broadening their experiences. At the same time, we rarely question suburban or urban students who lack a basic understanding of the communities unlike their own. I appreciate how Dr. Ardoin has captured the voices and perspectives of rural students' "hope, dreams, and realities." I respect her approach in offering the choice dilemmas rural students face when they consider college.

I not only found my way to college but also ended up earning three college degrees. I now study, teach, and write about the experiences of students in college as a faculty member. My story may seem unique to those reading this book and to the many who attended a high school with a college-going culture. Yet, my story is likely very similar to many high school students, including the ones in this book. There were no advanced placement or honors courses, no options for language courses or electives beyond industrial arts, no visits from college personnel, and, in fact, for some the opportunity to attend high school at all was a blessing. Dr. Ardoin pushes us to examine and contemplate the rural student and suggests much can be done to support this group. I share many of Dr. Ardoin's personal experiences about growing up in a rural area and had the pleasure of guiding her dissertation, much of which is included in this book. Dr. Ardoin shattered every myth about rural students in college and became the first Ph.D. student in the Higher Education Administration program at NC State. I am grateful we continue our educational journal together. Although scholars and policymakers are wrestling with how to best define rural, for anyone who lives in a rural area, we know exactly who we are. Dr. Ardoin's book helps others know about us too.

Audrey J. Jaeger, Ph.D.
Alumni Distinguished Graduate Professor and Professor of Education
NC State University

Acknowledgements

I am filled with gratitude for the opportunity to share this research and the stories of those who participated. This book would not have come to fruition without the following individuals:

First and foremost, the participants (and places) of this study. I am forever grateful for your willingness to share your experiences and stories with me and, now, with us. I hope I have represented you justly and I hope that you realize your own definitions of success.

My dissertation chair and mentor: Dr. Audrey Jaeger. You believed in this research and you believed in me. This is not only my labor but also yours.

My dissertation committee: Drs. Joy Gayles, Paul Umbach, and Lance Fusarelli. I appreciate your time, feedback, and challenge in the dissertation research process that led to this publication.

The series editors: Drs. Victoria (Tori) Svoboda and Buffy Smith. Thank you for reading my dissertation and encouraging me to progress it into a publication to be read and utilized by others.

Lexington Books staff: Nicolette Amstutz and Jessica Thwaite. Your assistance through this process was integral to moving this book from an idea to a reality.

Manuscript peer reviewers: (whoever you two are). I appreciate your time and feedback which challenged me to consider new perspectives and enhance the quality of this work.

My parents: Evelyn Ardoin and Steven Ardoin. You let me move back in at 30 so I could finish my degree, conduct research, and write. Your sacrifices have allowed me to pursue new paths.

My maternal grandparents: Lennis and Dorothy Guillory. I wish that y'all could see this! The counselor's pseudonym is in your honor because no one taught me to value education more than the two of you.

And last, but certainly not least, Zeb Jenkins, who is gracious about me using weekends for writing and who supports me fully and unequivocally. You are the definition of a true partner.

Author's Note

The essence of rural places is the small community atmosphere where everybody tends to know everybody else, including their stories. As such, to preserve participant confidentiality, this book combines the research data of the two rural, public high schools into one site—MapDot High School—merging the data from the two counselor participants into one pseudonym—Ms. Guillory—and the data from the eight students into two pseudonyms—Taylor and Landry. More information on the individual participants can be found in the Introduction of this book within the research methodology section.

Introduction

Rural Research Reasoning

WHAT IS RURAL?

Good question! In some ways, rural is a "know it when you see it" concept because there are no fixed definitions of rural or rurality (Flora, Flora, & Gasteyer, 2016; Flora, Flora, Spears, & Sawnson, 1992; Ganss, 2016; Isserman, 2005). For example, Tieken (2014) offers that rurality is a matter of "commonplace interactions and events" that are "tied to place . . . and sense of belonging" and give meaning to people who live in rural areas and identify their communities as rural (p. 5). It is estimated that the U.S. rural population was 46.2 million, or 14%, in 2015 (USDA Economic Research Service [ERS], 2016).

Tieken's conceptualization is one among many of rural and rurality. From traditional, operational definitions of rural that focus on place and demographics to newer code-based definitions—such as the rural-urban continuum classification codes, categorizations of rural vary by governmental branch, time period, scholars, and the media (Flora et al., 2016; Flora et al., 1992; Tieken, 2014). The US government defines rurality in six different ways: 1) U.S. Census Bureau, 2) Metropolitan status codes, 3) Urban-Rural continuum codes, 4) Metro-centric locale codes, 5) Urban-centric locale codes, and 6) Core-based statistical codes (U.S. Department of Education [DOE] Institute of Education Sciences [IES], 2007). Communities can be categorized differently depending on the chosen definition and regional variation. The U.S. DOE's IES (2007) offers that "population density, geographic features, and level of economic and industrial development" can all be rurality indicators (U.S. DOE IES, 2007, p. 4). Sociologists also utilize varying markers of rurality, including population size, distance from urban centers, homogenous cultures, natural resource economies, and unique identities (Flora et al., 2016).

Defining rural is further complicated because the U.S. government and rural sociologists often fluctuate between using the terms urban and rural and using the terms metropolitan and nonmetropolitan. Either way, rural/nonmetropolitan is often defined as a residual; in other words, it is everything that is not urban/metropolitan (Brown & Swanson, 2003; Flora et al., 2016; Flora et al., 1992; Tieken, 2014).

Examples of the complexities of rural definitions are showcased in the USDA ERS metropolitan and nonmetropolitan map, changing metro status map, and rural areas map in Appendices A, B, and C, respectively; rural places are located in light grey areas on each map. The U.S. Census Bureau also provides statistics that show the rural nature of various communities, including the site of this case study (see Appendix D). Regardless of which definition or measure is used, the rurality of this book's study site is affirmed by the U.S. government in every conceptualization of the rural term.

THE STATE OF RURAL SCHOOL SYSTEMS

The U.S. DOE's National Center for Education Statistics (NCES) (2013) reports that 50% of high schools are in rural areas, which accounts for "57% of school districts and 12 million students, representing 24% of total public, U.S. school enrollment" (p. 1–3). Rural district enrollments are also growing at faster rates than urban districts (as cited in Ganss, 2016). These statistics highlight how rural schools serve an important function within the broader U.S. educational system, educating almost one-fifth of U.S. elementary and secondary school students.

The Positives

Historically, rural schools are characterized by their unique attributes and connections to their communities, frequently serving as central places for the rural community to interact, host events, and create a sense of belonging (Tieken, 2014). Many rural communities depend on their schools to honor their history, unite their people, bolster their economy, rally their spirit, and, ultimately, differentiate their community from the next one down the road. Tieken (2014) describes rural schools as an identity, or heartbeat "providing shared symbols and traditions, perpetuating a set of common values, and establishing clear boundaries" (p. 65). While it may seem petty or erroneous to attribute so much value to schools, Carr and Kefalas (2009) emphasize "the ferocious love that inhabitants feel for their dots on the map" (p. viii) and, for many rural residents, those dots are often defined by their school.

Rural schools have many positive attributes. School administrators and teachers are often native to the rural community, believing it is a "special place," and providing parents and students with a sense of "continuity, unity, safety, and care" through their "knowledge of students' families and backgrounds" (Schafft & Jackson, 2010, p. 86). Rural schools are also typically smaller in size, which research shows create better academic and social environments for students (Ganss, 2016; Theobald & Siskar, 2008).

The Challenges

Despite their community value and positive elements, rural schools face many challenges. The social class status of many rural communities tends to be poor and working class—even more so than in urban areas; Johnson, Showalter, Klein, and Lester (2014) report that two out of five rural students live in poverty, a rate which is consistently growing. These economic realities result in lower tax revenues and lower property taxes, which impact public school funding and often leave rural schools with inadequate financial resources (Theobald & Siskar, 2008). These economic challenges can also make it difficult for rural schools to attract "outsiders" as teachers and administrators because of low salaries and, correspondingly, lack of interest. An absence of outsiders often creates an insulated environment and limits the range of perspectives to which rural students are exposed. Restricted access to goods, entertainment, and technological innovation also contribute to PK-12 school challenges (Theobald & Siskar, 2008). Regardless, rural schools are expected to meet national standards and provide similar opportunities to their suburban and urban counterparts without the same tax bases, grant programs, facilities, and access to human and public resources.

The numerous challenges rural schools face gives them a reputation of being inadequate (Theobald & Siskar, 2008). Rural schools' experience resource inequities, lack "the right kind of students," and are unable to offer certain kinds of curricula such as honors, advanced placement, and international baccalaureate courses (Jencks, 1972, p. 37; McDonough, Gildersleeve, and Jarsky, 2010; USDA ERS, 2003). Rural schools are also less likely to receive information about higher education and admissions requirements, particularly any changes that occur (McDonough et al., 2010).

Some scholars, such as Kelly (2009), even view rural schools as "places of great loss—of people, natural resources, and any vision of long-term viability" (p. 2). Outmigration is used as a tool for upward mobility—leaving the community to seek out "better lives" (Carr & Kefalas, 2009; Corbett, 2009; Flora et al., 2016; Kelly, 2009; McDonough et al., 2010; Tieken, 2014). Rural schools, particularly since the twentieth century, have become a means of "saving talented youth and sending them on to [other] places" where they will be offered what are seen—accurately or not—as countless opportunities (Thebold & Siskar, 2008, p. 294). This becomes an issue of "brain drain" for rural communities, when young, talented, and intelligent individuals depart the community for better education, job, and salary opportunities and never return home (Carr & Kefalas, 2009; Corbett, 2007; Theobald & Siskar, 2008; Tieken, 2014; USDA ERS, 2003). These rural students are encouraged by family and educators to "go far" or "get out," both implying the necessity of leaving the community for other places with seemingly better prospects (Flora et al., 2016: Theobald & Siskar, 2008, p. 293; Tieken, 2014, p. 115). In this way, rural schools can be viewed as "a functional meritocracy . . . or alternatively as totalizing social class reproduction machines" (Corbett, 2009, p. 2). Rural schools often teach and support social class reproduction by informing their students of standardized routines, norms, and knowledge that let students know "what they can expect to achieve [or not achieve] for themselves," particularly if they remain in their community (Corbett, 2007, p. 48–49). For many rural students, success in their communities means leaving, although encouraging the "best and brightest" to leave could result in further population and community decline (Carr & Kefalas, 2009; Tieken, 2014).

McDonough, Gildersleeve, and Jarsky (2010) share how many rural communities perceive higher education, particularly the four-year context, as "leaving home . . . leaving the ways of [rural] living in which one is raised" (p. 203). Corbett (2007) explored the issue of rural students' leaving or staying, considering "how some rural students 'learn to leave' while others 'learn to stay'" (p. 9). The Canadian Province in his study associated education with migration and identified a strong connection between learning and leaving. Rural Canadian youth often faced a significant and traumatic decision about whether to remain in the community or pursue postsecondary education elsewhere (Corbett, 2007). The link between education and community departure was "for some students . . . liberating, for others unthinkable, and for most it is problematic and conflicted" (Corbett, 2007, p. 18). This is another example of rural "brain drain" and the tension and emotional impact it may generate for both rural students and communities.

Despite the complexities rural schools face, the field of education often focuses on the plight of urban schools, all but ignoring the persistent challenges—including poverty, substance abuse, transience, test bias, and threats of closure—faced by rural communities, schools, and students (Tieken, 2014). Inequitable access on the basis of place is now being considered as a dimension of unequal educational opportunity (Corbett, 2009); this inequity manifests as lower levels of higher education aspiration, attendance, and choice for students from rural schools (Hu, 2003).

RECOGNIZING RURAL STUDENTS

For the purposes of this book and the study that informs it, rural students are defined as students from rural areas who are members of working-class families and would be the first person in their families to attend college, meaning their parents or guardians did not have any higher education experience at either two-year or four-year institutions. It is important to note that not all rural students identify in this way; some may come from affluent families, have parents who have attended higher education and/or earned degrees, or both. However, the population of this study, and thus this book, embodies the intersection of all three of these identities; so, when the phrase "rural students" is used anywhere in this text, it is referring to rural, working-class, and first-generation college students. I chose to study the intersection of these three identities in order to better understand the holistic experiences of rural, working-class, first-generation college students because much of the existing literature only focused on one or two of these identities but not all three in combination.

Rural students have many issues to contend with when considering higher education including but not limited to academic, information, financial, and role model constraints (Bergerson, Heiselt, & Aiken-Wisneiwski, 2013; Byun, Irvin, & Meece, 2012; Griffin, Hutchins, & Meece, 2011). Consequently, rural students are significantly underrepresented in higher education. Nationally, only 33% of individuals in rural areas enroll in higher education, compared to 48% of those in cities and 43% in suburban areas, and the gap is only widening (Brown & Swanson, 2003; Kusmin, 2011; McDonough et al., 2010; NCES, 2011). Hurst (2012) notes that "anecdotally, 3% has become a figure used widely to describe college [degree] attainment for [individuals from] the working class" (p. 26), which is likely one of the reasons Porterfield (2017) asserted that "expanding college access for rural students is a national [U.S.] imperative" and doing so would be beneficial not only for the rural students themselves but also "for our communities, our economy, and our country" (para. 1).

For many rural students, going to college is an "alien" concept and experience. There may be few college graduates in their rural areas; students may have never seen a college campus; and there are likely numerous unanswered questions and doubts about how to navigate the application process (Byun et al., 2012; Carr & Kefalas, 2009; Sacks, 2007; Pappano, 2017). Rural students are apprehensive about colleges and universities expecting them to change who they are and what they believe in order to truly become "educated" and they are concerned that they will never be able return home again—or see home in the same way—once they become educated (Carr & Kefalas, 2009; McDonough et al., 2010; Pappano, 2017).

The aforementioned trepidations may be, in part, because rural students tend to be members of families and communities that devalue theoretical learning and overvalue practical knowledge and application (Bergerson et al., 2013; Flora et al., 2016: Pappano, 2017; Willis, 1977). Rural parents often steer their children to consider full-time jobs, military service, or trade-based education right after high school, rather than higher education (Carr and Kefalas, 2009; Pappano, 2017). There is a focus in rural areas on the value of a steady income and family relationships over "fancy" careers; in other words, what is known to be actually possible instead of the vague promises that higher education offers (Archer, 2003b; Flora et al., 2016; McDonough et al., 2010). Pappano (2017) notes that, even when rural students express interest in academics, they are frequently steered toward career pathways that seem evident in their rural communities. Similar to the urban students in MacLeod's (2009) study, rural students often think about their employment in terms of blue-collar jobs, most of which do not require a college degree. However, regional economic challenges and a corresponding decline in blue-collar industries—such as farming, mining, manufacturing, and oil—may have rural students depending on jobs that will no longer be available (Pappano, 2017). Unsurprisingly, a middle-class lifestyle does not seem attainable to many rural students.

Compared to their middle- and upper-class peers, rural students may not see the same worth in formal education or feel they have as much access to it. Accordingly, rural students may be less academically prepared and less inclined to aspire to higher education due to a variety of factors including socioeconomic status (SES) and social class background, low educational attainment in families, and a limited number of community members with college degrees. Even if, or when, rural students do access and enroll in higher education, they are more likely to attend less selective or prestigious institutions and are less likely to persist to graduation than their middle- and upper-class peers (Walpole, 2003). Rural students often possess a "community college mentality" and they attend community colleges at a rate of 33.1% versus their urban and suburban peers' rates of 27.1% and 29.3%, respectively (Hu, 2003; McDonough et al., 2010). Bruni (2015) notes that "the [higher education] gap between the haves and the have nots has widened, raising the stakes of which side of the divide you wind up on" (p. 198).

Further, scholars, such as McDonough, Gildersleeve, and Jarsky (2010), call for more attention on rural schools, rural students, and rural college access in research, policy, and outreach. They point out the gap in research on "the *qualitative differences in educational opportunity* for rural students" and encourage researchers to focus their understanding on how rural cultures and students interrelate with higher education and identifying ways that higher education might better meet the needs of rural students (p. 193, emphasis in original).

WHY I CARE ABOUT RURAL STUDENTS

Heightened attention on rural students is important to me both personally and professionally. Identifying as first-generation college student from a working-class family who grew up in a rural area, I personally experienced mixed signals about my college aspirations, challenges in accessing higher education, and struggles with learning the new college language, which was full of jargon and acronyms. Conversely, I relished the opportunity to represent my family and community in my accomplishments as a college student and to share my rural, working-class perspective with my peers, advisors, and professors. The moment that symbolized my experiences as a rural, first-generation, working-class college student was on my undergraduate commencement day. My PawPaw held my diploma, appreciated a few moments of silence, then said, with a voice full of emotion, "I never thought I would get to hold one of these in my lifetime." I still want to cry when I think about it. My degree was not only about me; it was about all of the other rural, working-class individuals—my PawPaw included—who had the aptitude and desire to pursue higher education but were unable to overcome the barriers to college access. I became one of the 3% of working-class folks who earned a college degree in their lifetime (Hurst, 2012) and I believe it is my responsibility to represent my rural people.

These personal experiences fueled my research interests as I pursed graduate studies and further realized that not many "people like me" were represented in the student, staff, or faculty ranks at U.S. colleges and universities, particularly at four-year institutions. In fact, the U.S. higher education system was historically set up to keep "people like me" out and, as such, can still be complex to navigate for rural, first-generation, and working-class folks, individually and at the intersections. As an educator and scholar, I have not only observed the practical challenges that rural students face getting to and through higher education but also the gaps in exploring and examining experiences of rural students and the communities they call home in the higher education literature. Particularly, rural students are often overlooked in the college access and success literature. As such, I conducted research to address one aspect of the gaps—how rural, working-class, first-generation college students obtain college knowledge and decode university jargon as a component of their college access. My goal was to describe the college-going culture in one rural community, through the particular stories of tenth-grade public high school students and their high school counselors, in order to share suggestions about how to improve college access. It is my hope that these suggestions can transfer to other rural, working-class communities.

RESEARCH STUDY METHODOLOGY

Qualitative methods were chosen for this study because the purpose was to understand how and why rural students use various processes and resources to obtain and comprehend college knowledge and decode university jargon, which aligns well with qualitative research's purpose of understanding how people construct, interpret, and make meaning of their experiences in context (Creswell, 2007; Hesse-Biber & Leavy, 2011; Merriam, 2009; Mertens, 2010). Qualitative research also intends to give voice to underrepresented students and this study did that by giving voice to rural students, who are particularly underrepresented in higher education (Creswell, 2007; Merriam, 2009). The research design incorporated fieldwork, observations, subjectivity, analysis and synthesis, and researcher consciousness (Stake, 1995).

As a qualitative researcher, I assumed the role of research instrument in this study, constructing the questions and probes for interviews, creating the observation protocol, and obtaining and analyzing all necessary documents (Creswell, 2007; Merriam, 2009; Mertens, 2010). Principally, I served as an observer-participant, which means I made the purpose of my presence known to participants and interacted when necessary but did not attempt to disrupt or fundamentally alter any situations (Gold, 1958, as cited in Merriam, 2009; Mertens, 2010). This stance, along with my familiarity with the rural community as a frequent visitor, allowed me to obtain insider information while maintaining some outside perspective (Yin, 2009).

Descriptive Case Study Approach

A case study is an "in-depth description and analysis of a bounded system [or multiple bounded systems]" (Merriam, 2009, p. 40). Case studies allow for more selective sampling strategies, employ multiple methods of data collection, and provide a richer understanding of the topic through rich, thick description (Merriam, 2009; Mertens, 2010), focusing on both the particulars and the complexity, the uniqueness and commonality, of cases within certain circumstances (Hesse-Biber & Leavy, 2011; Merriam, 2009; Mertens, 2010; Stake, 1995).

Case studies use stories to explain and understand a concept and represent unique perspectives (Stake, 1995), which means they not meant to be generalizable, but, rather, seek to know a particular case well, with the main focus on understanding that specific case (Stake, 1995). Applied fields, such as education, often utilize case study for research (Merriam, 2009), seeking to:

- "retain the holistic and meaningful characteristics of real-life events" (Yin, 2009, p. 4),
- answer "how or why questions" (Yin, 2009, p. 9), and
- use "a full variety of evidence—documents, artifacts, interviews, and observations" (Yin, 2009, p. 11).

Specifically, this study was a collective, or multiple, case study. The advantage to collective case studies is that they are "often considered more compelling, and the overall study is therefore regarded as being more robust" (Merriam, 2009; Yin, 2009, p. 53). In collective case studies, each individual case study is deemed its own study; the individual cases are analyzed first, then the cases are synthesized collectively in a cross-case format (Merriam, 2009; Yin, 2009).

Case studies develop knowledge differently in four important ways: "1) more concrete, 2) more contextual, 3) more developed by reader interpretation, and 4) based more on reference populations determined by the reader" (Merriam, 2009, pp. 44–45). This case study aligned with Merriam's points as follows:

1. concrete knowledge—readers who share participants' identities can relate with participants' stories because data is shared in a lively, realistic, and relatable manner;
2. contextual knowledge—participants' stories are rooted in context, which allows for more practical knowledge and application;
3. interpretive knowledge—readers can layer their own experiences with the participants' stories to interpret the data; and
4. reference population knowledge—readers can take the case study data and apply it to a reference population in their own community.

In this sense, case studies allow for multiple realities to exist, even when those realities of the same concept are contradictory (Mertens, 2010; Stake, 1995).

Research Site and Participants

The sites and sample for this study were chosen based on criterion and purposive sampling strategies (Creswell, 2007; Krathwohl, 2009; Merriam, 2009; Mertens, 2010; Patton, 2002). Site selection criteria included the public high school's location in a rural county in the southeastern region of the

United States, the U.S. Census data on the town in which the high school was located, accessibility of the school, and the school district and public high school's willingness to participate in the study (Krathwohl, 2009; Mertens, 2010). These criteria followed Stake's (1999) counsel that "time and access for fieldwork are almost always limited . . . we need to pick cases which are easy to get to and hospitable to our inquiry" (p. 4).

Bound within one county's public high school district, rural high school tenth-graders and their rural high school counselors served as the individual cases, or participants, in the study. The district's school board was contacted, permission to conduct research was granted, and gatekeepers from each of the two high schools assisted with the study. Participants were identified through purposeful, criterion sampling with the assistance of the high school counselors; all participants lived in the rural county, professed college aspirations, received free or reduced lunch (which served as the marker for social class identity), and would be the first person in their family to attend college.

As shown in Table 1.1, two rural, public high schools served as sites for this study, with four tenth-grade students and one counselor participating at each site. To preserve participant confidentiality, this book combines the two rural, public high schools into one site, merging the data from the two counselors into one pseudonym and the data from the eight students into two pseudonyms.

Data Collection

Data was collected through interviews, observations, document analysis, field notes, and a self-reflective journal, providing appropriate triangulation for the collective case study (Merriam, 2009; Yin, 2009). Two semi-structured and additional informal interviews gathered information on the community and school habitus, perceptions of college value, exposure to university jargon and academic discourse, and processes used by both participants and community members to understand college knowledge and university jargon. Guidance meetings, with a focus on college counseling, and general school culture were observed. In addition, a variety of documents were analyzed including the public high schools' handouts about college, the district's available

Table 1.1 Study Participants

Public High School #1	Public High School #2
Student #1—White Woman	Student #5—Black Woman
Student #2—White Man	Student #6—White Man
Student #3—Black Woman	Student #7—White Man
Student #4—Black Man	Student #8—Biracial Woman
Counselor #1—White Woman	Counselor #2—White Woman

information on students' college attendance rates, and local colleges' and universities' admissions materials and websites.

Data Analysis

Data review and reflection was an ongoing, cyclical process with data collection (Hesse-Biber & Leavy, 2011; Krathwohl, 2009; Merriam, 2009; Mertens, 2010; Stake, 1995). Individual case analysis and cross-case synthesis was used to analyze the data; open and axial coding were employed to generate codes, themes and, ultimately, findings. Readers will see thick description utilized in this book—through portrayals of the community, public high schools, and participants—to illustrate the study's findings (Creswell, 2007; Krathwohl, 2009; Merriam, 2009; Mertens, 2010; Stake, 1995). Findings and implications from the study (see Chapters 4–7) address how rural students and their counselors view college access—particularly college knowledge and university jargon—and offer ideas to assist rural students and counselors in obtaining cultural capital, navigating college knowledge, and decoding university jargon.

Trustworthiness and Limitations

A critical component to trustworthiness is maximizing accurate representation of participants' perspectives in the study (Stake, 1995). Appropriate methods of trustworthiness—such as pseudonyms, significant time in the field, triangulating data, peer review, researcher reflexivity, and thick description—were incorporated to address credibility, dependability, transferability, and confirmability (Creswell, 2007; Hesse-Biber & Leavy, 2011; Merriam, 2009; Mertens, 2010; Stake, 1995; Yin, 2009). As qualitative research, this case study is meant to be transferable, rather than generalizable. Transferability is about "fittingness," or the process of applying the cases in one study to understand other similar, congruent cases (Lincoln & Guba, 2000a, as cited in Hesse-Biber & Leavy, 2011, p. 262). Other rural high schools and communities that have similar populations and context can transfer the descriptive analysis of the findings to their own unique context (Creswell, 2007; Merriam, 2009; Mertens, 2010; Stake, 1995). However, because this case study focused on one rural community in the southeastern region of the United States and framed college access through the narrow lens of college knowledge and, even more specifically, university jargon, this study was not designed to transfer to all rural, public high schools, all rural communities, nor to answer the larger question of how to increase overall access to postsecondary education for all rural students. Findings should be utilized with thoughtfulness to community and regional context to understand rural students' processes of decoding university jargon and constructing college knowledge.

OVERVIEW OF THE BOOK

The site and participants of this collective case study are described in chapter 1. Thick description of a rural, working-class community—referred to as MapDot, USA—is provided, including its public high school—Map-Dot High; two rural, working-class student representatives—Taylor and Landry; and a rural high school counselor representative—Ms. Guillory. These vignettes highlight the community environment, school context and offerings, and backgrounds of the case study participants. Both strengths and struggles of the rural community of MapDot, USA, are featured.

The college access gap for rural students is the focus of chapter 2, highlighting the challenges rural, working-class students face when trying to access higher education, including the college planning and application process, university recruitment and admissions practices, financial aid, and college knowledge.

The purpose of chapter 3 is to define and provide the major principles of Hossler and Gallagher's (1987) college choice model, Bourdieu's (1977) concepts of cultural capital and habitus, and college access, specifically college knowledge and university jargon. Explanations of the link between cultural capital and college access in the predisposition and search stages of college choice are featured. Connections between the model and college-going practices are also examined.

The paradoxical ways in which rural communities perceive higher education is demonstrated in chapter 4. Information about local belief systems, typical occupational paths, the financial climate, and the limited ability to obtain outside experiences or perspectives is included. Attention is given to the mixed signals that rural, working-class students receive from their families and communities about pursing higher education, despite students' hopes and dreams.

Rural students share their challenges with college aspiration and access in chapter 5, particularly related to college knowledge and university jargon, and what steps they take to bridge the rural higher education gap. Common postsecondary educational aspirations of rural students are highlighted and three specific steps that rural, working-class students utilize in their college knowledge acquisition are showcased, including: (1) becoming aware, (2) recognizing and defining terms, and (3) finding processes of seeking and understanding information.

Experiences of rural, public high school counselors' mentality and challenges around the multiple roles and responsibilities required in their position are shared through the story of Ms. Guillory in chapter 6. The realities faced by Ms. Guillory are compared to the opportunities other types of schools have to employ full-time counselors devoted to only college-prep.

Finally, insights into how all people involved in education can influence rural, working-class students from their respective platforms is offered in chapter 7. Individuals with postsecondary experience living in rural communities are encouraged to volunteer with their local schools and mentor students. Public high schools and their districts are challenged to create or fund professional development opportunities for counselors and share more college knowledge with families. Higher education is urged to simplify and expand their rural recruitment and admissions practices. Policymakers are called to consider the benefit of expanding, or at least maintaining, the presence of high school counselors in rural environments. Scholars and researchers are encouraged to explore more rural issues. The reality that everyone impacts the college predisposition and search phases of rural, working-class students is highlighted.

Chapter 1

Rural Representation

While statistics are clear that rural, working-class public schools send fewer students to college and rural students are less likely to aspire to and access higher education than their suburban and urban peers, those statistics do not represent the complete picture of college-going in rural areas (Brown & Swanson, 2003; Kusmin, 2011; McDonough, Gildersleeve, & Jarsky, 2010; National Center for Education Statistics [NCES], 2011). The experiences of rural students, public schools, and communities are best told by those who live the experience. MapDot, USA, its public high schools—the sites of this case study, and the students who attend it—the study participants—exhibit many of the rural issues which constrain college aspirations and access, but the rural students also challenge the stereotypes of their schools and communities by viewing themselves as both college-ready and college-bound. It is communities like MapDot and individual students' and educators' stories of resistance and resilience that should represent rural schools and communities more often in the educational literature.

It is important to reiterate here (as in the Introduction) that MapDot is one rural community in the southeastern region of the United States. This case study of MapDot was designed to share its particulars and, thus, the study of MapDot may not transfer to all rural communities, public high schools, or for all rural students and high school counselors. However, it is my belief that other rural folks, particularly those who identify as working-class college students and first-generation college students, can—and will—see elements of their own communities and stories within the case study of MapDot.

Additionally, readers should note that, to preserve participant confidentiality, this book combines the research data of the two rural, public high schools into one site—MapDot High School, merging the data from the two counselor participants into one pseudonym—Ms. Guillory—and the data from the eight students into two pseudonyms—Taylor and Landry. More information on the individual participants can be found in the Introduction of this book within the research methodology section.

WELCOME TO MAPDOT, USA

If you take a sparse exit off of a secluded area of the interstate highway and drive 30 miles west, you will arrive in the farmlands that residents of Map-Dot, USA call home. The rural county is comprised of a small city, several towns, and some bedroom communities, some with official incorporations and zip codes, and others that are just known as separate places to locals. In every direction you look, you will see open land—fields of cotton, soybeans, rice, and cattle.

There is a Wal-Mart in the county seat 10 miles away from MapDot, but you will have to drive at least an hour to locate the nearest shopping mall or major chain restaurant. With the exception of some fast food franchises, most of what you will find here are local businesses—mom and pop shops that have existed for decades and are being passed down through families. Entertainment primarily consists of youth and high school sporting events, hunting and fishing, annual festivals celebrating aspects of the local culture, churches happenings, and visiting with family, friends, and neighbors. Some would call it a slow pace in an out of touch place. Others would say it is the best way to live—rural.

A Snapshot of MapDot's County

MapDot is located in a small, rural county that has seen a declining population over the past ten years (U.S. Census Data, 2015). The residents are approximately 70% White, with Black/African American as the largest underrepresented racial group at 29% (U.S. Census Data, 2015). Only 68% of the county's population has a high school diploma and 12% have a bachelor's degree, in contrast to national averages of 86% and 29%, respectively (U.S. Census Data, 2015). This marks MapDot as one of the lowest education counties on the USDA Economic Research Service (ERS) map on low-education counties, shown in dark black (see Appendix E). The median household income is $30,323 compared to a national average of $53,482, with 24% of persons falling below the poverty line compared to a national average of 13.5% (U.S. Census Data, 2015); this puts MapDot in the dark black, or most impoverished counties, category on the USDA ERS persistent poverty counties map (see Appendix F).

The majority of residents in the county tend to find employment through occupational fields including but not exclusively limited to the oil field, medical field, small and local business, clerical work, law enforcement, farming, and K-12 education. Residents' roles in these occupational fields are generally classified as poor or working-class jobs because of the manual labor, higher risks, lower incomes, and minimal training or education (Flora et al., 2016). Despite these potential challenges, like many rural communities, MapDot's county is known to have low crime rates, significant natural resources, and the feeling of a close-knit, collaborative community (Theobald & Siskar, 2008; USDA ERS, 2003).

MapDot County's Public School District

The State Department of Education ranked MapDot county's school district near the middle of its sixty-two school districts, making it an "average" public school district in the state (State Department of Education, 2011a). The district consists of five public high schools. Four of the public high schools are traditional high schools that offer students two academic paths—the college-bound path and the career path (explained below in the academic curriculum section)—through which they can earn their high school diploma (State Department of Education, 2012). The fifth public high school is an alternative high school that is not counted by the state in the county graduation rates because the school only grants students the general education development (GED) certificate. Academically, the four traditional, public high schools in MapDot's district did not offer any specialized programs or courses, such as International Baccalaureate (IB) degrees and Advanced Placement (AP) courses at the time of the study (State Department of Education, 2011b). The 2011 school performance letter grades given to public schools in the district ranged from B to D (State Department of Education, 2011a). MapDot county's public high schools fell in the middle of the district's school performance letter grades.

The district's four traditional, public high schools varied in their total enrollment, ranging in number from 400 to 850 students (State Department of Education, 2011b). Racial diversity and graduation rates of the district's public high schools also varied widely. One of the four public high schools was 75% African American and had the lowest graduation rate at 59.6%, while one of the majority White public high schools had the highest graduation rate at 92.7% (County School Board, 2010). The two MapDot county public high schools in this study were more representative of the district's graduation rates at 67.2% and 74.5%, respectively (County School Board, 2010). The majority of the student population at each school in the MapDot district was considered "at-risk" based on students' social class status, which was marked by the 66% to 92% participation in the federal free/reduced lunch program (State Department of Education, 2011b). MapDot county and its public schools provide one example of rural secondary education in the United States and the barriers some rural, working-class students face when they aspire and attempt to access higher education.

MAPDOT HIGH SCHOOL

MapDot High School is located in one of the larger towns—MapDot—in the rural county; 55% of the residents identify as White and 43% identify as Black (U.S. Census Data, 2010). MapDot High has been serving this community since approximately 1921 and, at the time of this study, employed 25 teachers and one counselor and enrolled 450 high school students, 90 of whom were tenth-graders. Within the rural school district, MapDot High fell in the middle range for its enrollment numbers, school performance letter grade, 70% graduation rate, and approximately 10% dropout rate (State Department of Education, 2011b). Similar to other county public high schools, the majority of the student population was considered "at-risk" because approximately 80% of the students are enrolled in the federal free/reduced lunch program (State Department of Education, 2011b), indicating a poor or working-class social class status.

MapDot High consists of one main high school building that contains classrooms, administrative offices, restrooms, and the home economics studio and one secondary building that houses classrooms, the "shop class," and a computer lab. There is also a basketball gym (which lacks air-conditioning), a football field, and a small band building. At the time of the study, there was very limited technology in the MapDot High facilities; in fact, teachers often used transparencies and chalkboards during their classes. Most of the MapDot High facilities are in disrepair or outdated because the district has a minimal budget. To exacerbate facility issues, between 2010 and 2015, the school partially flooded and dealt with both mold and lead paint. Subsequently, MapDot High called and depended on parents and community members to assemble fundraising campaigns for facility repairs and updates. For example, a social media campaign was initiated by MapDot High supporters in an attempt to raise enough money over a five-year period to retrofit the gym with air-conditioning. This effort was not only to aid student-athletes and fans during athletic events but also because the gym served as a general meeting space and graduation location, even in weather over 100 degrees.

MapDot High students often begin their educational experience together as kindergarteners, although the public high school does also welcome in students from the PK-8 school one community over. The teachers and administrators typically know the students and their families well, often having educated older siblings, attended high school with parents, or established friendships with families. Tieken (2014) described such a school environment as a place where people are known, where every name is recognized, and where everyone gets attention. MapDot High is a "small school" environment, with all the advantages and obstacles of a close-knit community, including high levels of one-on-one attention as well as cliques and bullying. The counselor at MapDot High, Ms. Guillory, listed the following as the central issues for students: lack of resources (of all kinds, but particularly financial resources); lack of transportation, particularly for opportunities like dual enrollment with the local community college or any kind of postsecondary education; lack of support at home, including students' and parents' lack of college knowledge; lack of exposure to outside opportunities and perspectives; poor academic qualifications; and local and national employment and economic issues.

Academic Curriculum

At the time of the study, MapDot High School offered the three state-mandated academic tracks, including diploma and certification options for its students: 1) Core 4+ Academic Diploma Endorsement, 2) Core 4 Career/Technical Diploma Endorsement, and 3) Basic Core Certificate. All students were automatically placed on one of the Core 4 academic tracks during their ninth- and tenth-grade years of high school. However, after their tenth-grade year, students and parents had to decide, based on students' overall academic performance and post–high school aspirations, if the student would remain on a Core 4+ track, shift to the less rigorous Core 4 track, or move to Basic Core track. The timing of this decision made the tenth-grade year crucial for students at MapDot High because their academic track choice would determine if they would be eligible for college admission in their home state. State colleges and universities only accepted students who obtained a Core 4+ Academic Endorsement diploma. Despite known statistics on college-going and students' personal academic credentials, Ms. Guillory, the counselor, found that many students believed they were going to college, at least in the earlier years of high school.

Students' path to college was bumpy though. MapDot High did not offer any specialized academic programs or courses—such as international baccalaureate (IB) degrees and advanced placement (AP) courses, and the school performance letter grades imparted by the state tended to be in the C range (State Department of Education, 2011a). Recognizing its community and student population, MapDot High focused its curriculum on more vocational courses and pathways like home economics, agriculture, and "shop" to meet students' wants and potentially their future needs. This was an example of what Tieken (2014) posits about students in rural, working-class areas receiving a different type of education—one that prepares them for blue-collar jobs more common in their communities than higher education and professionalized career fields.

Extracurricular Opportunities

The after-school activities at MapDot High were mostly focused around athletics; the school boasted relatively successful programs in cross-country, track, football, basketball, baseball, softball, and cheerleading. The community showed strong support for the sports teams and one would often find the stands full of parents and community members clad in school colors during games. In addition, MapDot offered students opportunities to play an instrument in the band, act in one of two plays per year, or be a member or officer of student organizations such as Student Council, Future Farmers of America (FFA), Future Business Leaders of America (FBLA), 4-H Club, and French Club.

Students and Counselor

Taylor and Landry are two students at MapDot High School who identify as rural, poor or working-class, and potential first-generation college students. Their stories represent a sample of their rural peers, not only at their own public high school but also in the broader county's school district, who identify similarly. Their high school counselor, Ms. Guillory, is also a local of MapDot and she worked with Taylor and Landry for the duration of their elementary and secondary education experiences, giving her a holistic picture of their journeys. Ms. Guillory is one of the few resources from whom Taylor and Landry can learn more about higher education. It is important to note here that not all MapDot High students identify as poor or working-class, nor would all be the first in their family to pursue higher education; however, many MapDot High students do identify this way, as well as many rural students generally (Flora, Flora, & GasTeyer, 2016; Howley & Howley, 2010). A key framing of the vignettes of Taylor, Landry, and Ms. Guillory is that these are their individual stories, which may or may not be transferable to the stories of other rural, public high school students and counselors.

Meet Taylor

Taylor was a 15-year-old young woman who identified as Black, received federal free or reduced lunch, and resided in an even more remote area on the outskirts of MapDot, a location where she had spent her entire life. She was the oldest of three siblings and tended to spend quite a bit of time with her family. Academically, she enjoyed math while having some disdain for biology and French. Taylor was engaged in cocurricular activities; she was a member of the track and basketball teams and the cheerleading squad. She was known around MapDot High as a loud and boisterous young woman. In her free time, Taylor liked reading books about vampires and the apocalypse and hanging out with her friends.

Taylor's immediate and extended family was employed in jobs and fields typical of folks around MapDot such as law enforcement, farming, and entry-level ranks of the medical profession (e.g., licensed practical nurses or medical technical positions). Specifically, her father was a correctional officer at the local penitentiary and her mother was a pharmacy technician. Several members of her dad's side of the family were police officers. Taylor had two people in her life with college experience—a godmother who attended a state historically black college or university (HBCU) and her mother's godchild who attended the public, flagship university in the state's capital but did not complete his degree.

Attending college was definitely in Taylor's plans but mostly as a general concept. She did not have a specific career commanding her attention nor did she have a preference of what type of higher education institution to attend. However, Taylor was certain that she wanted an easy career which made "good money." She also knew that she would need to work while she attended college in order to afford higher education.

Meet Landry

Landry was a 16-year-old, White man and MapDot local who also received the federal free or reduced lunch program. Although he began his schooling at another public school in the county, where he completed his kindergarten and first-grade years, he transferred in the second grade to the elementary school that is tied to MapDot High. He noted that the only real difference between his two schools was that the first, prior school seemed to be a bit more academically challenging. Landry was one of five children in his family, with one older brother and three younger sisters. Academically, he gravitated toward math, science, and theater and often struggled with social studies. Landry was engaged in MapDot High as an athlete for the football and basketball teams. Outside of school activities, Landry was a self-proclaimed "simple guy" who enjoyed hunting and fishing and held down a part-time job at the local grocery store, where he mostly worked weekend hours.

The majority of folks in Landry's family found work in local businesses or the oil and agricultural fields. His father was a welder and drove a school bus; his mother was a local beautician; his stepmother was a clerk at a local furniture store; one grandfather worked for a local lumber store; and the other grandfather worked in the oil field. Landry's brother began the pursuit of a college degree with the intent to become a registered nurse; however, the brother later dropped out and found work in the oil field. With the exception of his brother's attempt, no one in Landry's immediate or extended family had ever been to college.

Landry planned to become to the first person in his entire family to succeed in higher education. He was hopeful that his athletic ability would provide him with access to scholarship funding since he knew his C-average grades would not likely earn him any merit-based financial aid; he longed to continue his football or basketball pursuits into, and after, college. However, Landry also had the "backup plan" to pursue a career in a technological field or physical therapy if his athletics pursuits faltered.

Meet Ms. Guillory

Ms. Guillory identified as a 50-something, White woman and a native of MapDot. Not only did she grow up in town, but she also returned here directly after her four years at college. In many ways, it was like she had never left. Ms. Guillory attended the county's only private high school before becoming the first person in her family to go to college. She attended a local, public state university to pursue a bachelor's degree in education, where she waffled between a major in elementary or secondary education but ended up choosing elementary education. Upon reflection about why she chose education as her career, Ms. Guillory commented that it was both "easy" and a "good fit" for her.

Ms. Guillory had spent her entire career employed at MapDot High School, beginning her work as an elementary school teacher. Through her teaching role she noticed that students seemed to lack a needed advocate; so, after five years of teaching, Ms. Guillory went back to graduate school to pursue her master's degree in counseling in hopes of becoming the first counselor at MapDot High. Her plan was successful and she continues to serve as the sole counselor at the public high school. The one major change Ms. Guillory has experienced in the past 30 years was the consolidation of the county's public schools. While MapDot High was not really impacted by the consolidation, other PK-12 schools either became PK-8 schools or had their middle grades moved to another school. Ms. Guillory mentioned how the closure of some public high schools in the county was met with much contempt from residents of those towns and fears about the loss of town identity (Tieken, 2014).

Outside of her counselor role, Mrs. Guillory is the mother of four children, all of whom attended MapDot High and then went on to pursue higher education at one of the state's public universities. She lives with her husband in a neighboring community approximately five miles from the public high school and is engaged in the community through church activities, a women's group, and cheering on MapDot High's sports teams.

CONCLUSION

MapDot, USA, is an example of a rural community where the public high school serves as the community lifeblood—binding people together, defining the community, and characterizing its dot on the map. Taylor, Landry, and Ms. Guillory's lived experiences of rurality serve as a representation of some rural students and the educators who serve them. Their experiences at MapDot High School, which are more fully explored in chapters 4–7, contribute insight on rural, public high school and community culture and how working-class, first-generation college students are encouraged or dissuaded from college-going, whether intentionally or unintentionally.

Chapter 2

The College Access Gap
for Rural Students

Geography and social class influence access to all educational opportunities—PK-12 and higher education—in the United States. Educational inequity begins with household factors such as income, parental educational attainment, and other social class identity markers—like rurality—that shape children's access to knowledge, materials, and experiences that promote learning and development. Carr and Kefalas (2009) suggest that "one's fate [is] set before they walk into kindergarten on the first day of school" (p. 33). It is a reality that different groups of people receive disproportionate amounts of the nation's educational resources, and these inequities have persisted and worsened over time (McDonough et al., 2010; Jencks, 1972). Where one lives—geography—and the financial, cultural, and social capital, all components of social class identity, in their proximity influences the types of educational institutions they can attend, which in turn impacts their access to curriculum, teachers, counselors, and, likely, future educational opportunities (Flora et al., 2016). Children in rural and working-class areas are taught information and behaviors that prepare them for blue-collar work; thus, scholars argue, schools perpetuate geographical and social stratification (Archer, 2003; McDonough et al., 2010; Tieken, 2014). Sacks (2007) also notes that class identity "defines the [U.S.] educational system" and "recreates the cultural norms of dominant social classes [and ideologies], expecting all students to succeed according to those rules" (p. 130 & 195).

Knowing higher education is not the path for many, scholars question the civic responsibility of U.S. public schools and whose interest they truly serve because of the public policy pressure to "teach to the test," which is a major component of college qualifications, rather than imparting lifelong skills such as critical thinking, problem solving, and genuine curiosity. Educators offer that making kids smart and helping them become college-ready are not always the same thing (Sacks, 2007). Standardized testing, which is known to be biased based on race, class, and even region, is often used as a measure of students' academic ability and college-readiness and a measure for schools' evaluation and funding, when, in fact, all these tests really do is reinforce wealth and power structures. Testing also "labels and sorts" students, which can lead students to "internalize these judgements of themselves . . . as being smart or not so smart" (Sacks, 2007, p. 99). The testing process also results in high school teachers, counselors, and administrators making clear delineations of who is potentially college-bound and who is likely never leaving the rural area, and, accordingly, those who are viewed as having potential are offered more opportunities (Carr and Kefalas, 2009).

In addition to questions about the PK-12 system, there is an ongoing debate about whether higher education is a public good, benefiting broader society, or a private good, only benefiting the individual student. Heller (2013) argues that it is not an either/or debate but really a both/and situation:

> as individuals invest in schooling beyond high school, they reap benefits in the form of higher wages and access to better careers (job autonomy, better benefits, and better working conditions) . . . and these individual investments benefit society though higher levels of economic growth, higher levels of tax collections, and lower levels of what are categorized as socially negative behaviors. (p. 96).

Perna (2013) cites additional public benefits of higher education including but not limited to a more skilled and adaptable workforce, higher labor force participation and employment rates, less reliance on social support programs, higher rates of civic engagement, and increased philanthropic giving. President Truman's Commission on Higher Education also acknowledged the public return on higher education back in 1947: "money expended for education is the wisest and soundest investment in the national interest" (as cited in Heller, 2013, p. 97). Viewing higher education as a public good and acknowledging the resulting benefits, there are frequent calls from scholars and activists to increase access to and success in higher education, particularly for students from underrepresented identities, including rural students (defined in this study as working-class, first-generation college students from rural communities). One of these calls is to recognize how the college planning and application process are inequitably designed—historically and presently, favor students from privileged identities, and serve as a barrier to rural students.

THE COLLEGE PLANNING AND APPLICATION PROCESS

The effects of the college planning and application process are most severe on students who lack familiarity with it, such as rural students.

Bruni (2015) shares that "fewer than 10% of children from families in the bottom quartile of income" will obtain a college degree by age 24, in contrast with "70% of children from families in the top quartile" (p. 119). Specifically, among the highest-ability students, 60% of the poor and working-class students attended college compared to 86% of the most affluent students. In addition, 34% of poor and working-class students with high test scores did not apply at all (Sacks, 2007). In short, students from the poor and working class are less likely to apply to or attend college than their peers (Cabrera & LaNasa, 2001; Griffin et al., 2011; McDonough, 1997). In part, this gap is related to the knowledge rural students have about higher education and if, or how, they can navigate the application process.

Many rural students often have unrealistic expectations about the process—particularly about the financial aid they are likely to receive—because they obtain much of their information anecdotally, rather than through official channels such as school counselors or college admissions offices, and they tend to hastily change their college aspirations, goals, and plans (Conley, 2005). First-generation college students are less likely to have the personal or institutional connections to assist them in obtaining information and support in the college planning process (Vargas, 2004). As such, rural students are less likely to take college entrance examinations (ACT/SAT); are less represented in courses or programs that often predict college enrollment such as honors courses, advanced placement (AP) courses, and international baccalaureate (IB) programs; and are less aware of courses required for college admission or grant aid programs (McDonough, 1997; Perna & Kurban, 2013; Vargas, 2004). While a rural student cannot control their access to a rigorous curriculum, they are still being judged on whether or not their high school offered one and whether or not they engaged in it. Sacks (2007) critiques higher education's obsession with these aforementioned high school "academic rigor" markers as "code for . . . sorting [students] by race and class" (p. 79).

Even when rural students are high-achieving with college aspirations, they face familial and community cultures that may constrain those aspirations. Studies of first-generation and rural students provide testaments about family resource differentiation, parents' lack of understanding of college knowledge, pervasive poverty in their hometowns, overwhelming aspects of higher education, and the conflict experienced between students' hometowns and higher education (Bickel, Banks, & Spatig, 1991; Flora et al., 2016; McDonough, 1997; O'Quinn, 1999; Simmons & Bryan, 2009). Additionally, rural students often assume that their parents would prefer for them not to attend college due to lack of overt support from their family and peer networks (James et al., 1999; O'Quinn, 1999).

Geography further complicates rural students' college-going as well (Bruni, 2015); higher education institutional proximity to students' rural hometowns can be a key factor, or limitation, for not only the students but also any family and friends who may be engaged in the college decision-making process. There is an ever-present question about how far from home they are allowed, or will allow themselves, to go (Flora et al., 2016; McDonough et al., 2010). In many cases, rural students determine "far" by time, rather than miles, and hope to be within a one- or two-hour radius of their hometowns in order to maintain connection to family and friends (McDonough, 1997). Geography can also relate to financial concerns because, rather than paying additional fees for room and board, rural students may try to cut costs by living at home and maintaining jobs they had during high school.

Bruni (2015) points out the "power of social privilege" in college admissions and how many students, families, and even, broadly, communities cannot afford the "unthinkable luxury" of applying to either multiple institutions, selective institutions, or both (p. 34 & p. 50). McDonough (1997) found that social class identity impacts the selectivity of a student's college choice twice as much as race or gender. This is why institutional competitiveness and selectivity are directly related to the social class identity of their student population; the more competitive and selective an institution, the more affluent its student body (Mullen, 2010). Subsequently, poor and working-class students are often concentrated in two-year community colleges and for-profit higher education institutions, which further highlights the stratification of students among institutional type by social class (Baum, Ma, & Payea, 2010; Mullen, 2010; Perna, 2013; Perna & Kurban, 2013; Sacks, 2007). This distinction is not because rural students do not academically qualify for admission to four-year or selective institutions; rather, these decisions are often based on lack of information about options, understanding of tuition and other costs, availability of financial aid, location of the institution, transportation, and proximity to home. Sacks (2007) notes that "where one goes to college continues to be dependent on one's circumstances at birth" (p. 127). Even when rural, working-class, and first-generation students do access higher education, they are often faced with "leaving behind their families . . . and [being] surrounded by affluent, culturally sophisticated, and highly competitive peers" (Sacks, 2007, p. 256).

College and University Recruiting and Admissions

To further complicate rural students' planning and application process, colleges and universities seem to have varying levels of interest in students based on the place students call home (Corbett, 2009). Institutions of higher education, particularly four-year colleges and universities, often send less information to rural schools and conduct less recruiting in rural areas. Aronson (2008) uses a funnel analogy to describe the diminishing access students from underrepresented groups have to education as they move through the ranks—high school to college to graduate or professional programs. Even with all the rhetoric about higher education valuing diversity—including social class and first-generation college student identities—and seeking greater diversity in student, staff, and faculty composition, many institutions tend to target recruitment efforts where they believe, or know, they will see the largest numerical returns—affluent, suburban schools and communities (Scherer & Anson, 2014). This may leave rural, working-class students feeling unwanted or devalued and perceiving colleges and universities as neither welcoming nor inviting.

Examining recruitment practices, Sacks (2007) reports that "among four-year public institutions . . . the single most heavily recruited group consisted of 'academically talented' students—invariably those students with high test scores from generally affluent circumstance" (p. 165). The subsequent institutional priorities included student-athletes, racial and ethnic minorities, and legacy students. Only 27% of public institutions and 24% of private institutions make an effort to recruit poor and working-class students (Sacks, 2007). McDonough (1997) appeals to admissions offices to "rethink their outreach" to rural, working-class students (p. 157).

Early Admissions Programs

Early admissions programs are a recruitment tactic at prestigious institutions of high education which desire to secure the first-year class long before the official application deadline in the spring and assure their yield rate, which is a factor in institutional rankings. Early admissions programs require students to apply for admission during the fall of their senior year—before they know about their financial aid options—and obligate students to enroll if they are admitted through the program (Soria, 2015). Many students in affluent areas, and particularly at private high schools, are encouraged to engage in early admissions programs in order to secure a spot at one of the "top institutions" in the United States. These programs are highly dependent on "insider information, involving a cozy alliance of privileged students, their guidance counselors at private prep schools, and college admissions officers at prestigious colleges" and, as such, there is a direct correlation between early admissions and social class background (Sacks, 2007, p. 148). There is no question that early admissions programs facilitate stratification of educational opportunities and may limit the seats in the first-year class that are available for rural students.

Legacy Admissions

In addition to early admissions programs, many colleges and universities also employ legacy admissions preferences. Legacy admission is when applicants get preferential treatment in the admissions process because of an existing tie to the institution—sons or daughters of alumni, relatives, or close friends of major donors, etc. (Mullen, 2010). Bruni (2015) highlights how this favoritism flourishes, particularly at selective institutions, which can limit rural students' access to college and universities. In fact, some institutions even have a practice of "development admits," which target students who come from very affluent families with whom the institution hopes to cultivate relationships for fundraising efforts (Sacks, 2007, p. 155). Legacy admissions are, obviously, only helpful to affluent students whose families have college educations and social connections. Very few, if any, rural students, as defined in this study, have the added benefit of being on legacy lists.

The Rankings Game

Admissions policies, particularly at selective institutions, are fueled by the measures used in college and university rankings, which heavily weigh selectivity, graduation rates, and reputation (Kamenetz, 2016). Selectivity scores are often calculated through application numbers, acceptance rates, yield rates, class ranks, and standardized test scores as measures of "quality" institutions (Bruni, 2015); graduation rates are based on how many students earn degrees within four years of enrolling, and reputation is based on perceptions of the institution from its peers, which is often a biased and faulty process (Kamenetz, 2016). Because rural, working-class, first-generation college students often have lower standardized test scores and face more hurdles in graduating within four years, increasing the number of rural students on campus can be in "stark contrast" to institutional goals—such as rankings (Warnock, 2016, p. 174). In fact, Sacks (2007) demonstrates that there is "often an inverse correlation between a university's commitment to [poor and working-class] students and its performance in the rankings game" (p. 135).

Diversity, of any kind, is not a consideration on how the U.S. News and World Report ranks institutions (Bruni, 2016). This is why we often see more privileged students from dominant identity groups in the most prestigious colleges and universities and underrepresented students clustered in community colleges and for-profit institutions (Warnock, 2016). Sacks (2007) chastises institutions for compromising diversity and equity for a prize in the "status and prestige . . . beauty contest" offered by organizations like the U.S. News and World Report that "reward the rich [students] and punish the poor [students]" (p. 129 & p. 132), and Bruni (2015) points out that the U.S. News and World Report rankings are not only debatable but also "fatally flawed" (p. 82).

Financial Aid

Perna (2013) notes that "money matters" in students' college planning and application processes and she considers financial aid and resources as one of her four predictors of college access and enrollment (p. 15), while Johnson and Strange (2005) cited financial issues as "the single strongest and most persistent threat to high student achievement" in rural communities (p. 6). Part of this threat is being able to navigate financial aid processes like the Free Application for Federal Student Aid (FAFSA). The FAFSA's seven-page long, 100-question form requires students and families to disclose their federal tax return information in order to determine the expected family contribution to the students' college-going costs and how much aid—through federal grants and loans—the student may receive (Heller, 2013). The FAFSA can produce many concerns for rural students whose parents do not submit tax returns or do not want to share their tax information, making this complex form another barrier to college access. However, completing the FAFSA is the only way students become eligible for Pell grants, some merit-based and need-based aid programs, and student loans—all of which are likely essential for rural students. Each financial aid resource is described below.

Pell Grants

Originally intended to cover almost all of the cost of college, the Basic Educational Opportunity Grant program—better known as the Pell Grant—was instituted through the passage of the Higher Education Act (HEA) of 1965 (Jones, 2013). In 1972, the Pell Grant covered almost 90% of public university costs and 40% of private university costs for families with incomes of less than $40,000 per year (Sacks, 2007). The percentage of costs covered has been slowly decreasing over time and, in 2004, the Pell Grant only covered 23% of total costs at public institutions and a measly 9% of total costs at private institutions (Sacks, 2007). In 2016, the Pell Grant award for an entire academic year was $5,775 (Goldrick-Rab, 2016). This decrease in the purchasing power of the Pell Grant means that the grant is just 15% of total financial aid packages and "nine out of ten Pell recipients graduate with debt" (Goldrick-Rab, 2016, p. 5; Sacks, 2007). This is a major concern because it is well known that grant aid is much more effective in ensuring college access than student loans, therefore making grant aid crucial for the college-going of underrepresented students, such as rural, working-class, first-generation college students (Heller, 2013).

Merit Aid vs. Need Aid

Federal and state aid programs are shifting their funding priorities from need-based aid to merit-based aid—or from aid based on family income and financial need to aid based on academic aptitude as measured by GPA and standardized test scores (Heller, 2013; Warnock, 2016). Merit aid is often granted to affluent students from "better" high schools, in effect providing advantages to "the very students who *don't* need the money for college—at the expense of those students who can't afford college without need-based financial aid" (Bruni, 2015; Heller, 2013; Sacks, 2007, p. 147, emphasis in original). The statistics that only 34% of public institutions and 27% of private institutions provide need-based aid highlights its scarcity (Sacks, 2007). Shifting aid from need-based to merit-based widens the access and success gap between affluent students and poor and working-class students.

States also award funding based on this myth of meritocracy. They have established state merit-based aid programs to provide grant funding to "high-achieving high school graduates . . . based solely on student academic achievement" (Hearn, Jones, & Kurban, 2013, p. 169). Programs such as Georgia's Helping Outstanding Pupils Educationally (HOPE) and Florida's Bright Futures, while intended to increase college-going within the state for underrepresented students, are providing hundreds of millions of dollars in merit-based funding to students who are typically from White, affluent families and more suburban high schools, which offer advancement placement and international baccalaureate courses and fare better on standardized test measures (Hearn et al., 2013; Heller, 2013). Sacks (2007) calls these programs "subsidies from the states to relatively affluent taxpayers, offered under the legitimating guise of academic merit" (p. 184). States with these large merit aid programs do not tend to give attention to other forms of aid with the assumption that these programs cover all students (Hearn et al., 2013). In addition, many of these programs are now facing budget issues and cuts due to state divestment in higher education (Warnock, 2016). While that may not be an issue for the affluent students receiving the aid whose families can cover the gap, it can mean the difference between retention or drop out for poor and working-class students who are heavily dependent on the aid.

Loans

Because of institutions' preference for merit-based aid, many financial aid packages shift to loans for higher education financing, which are known to dissuade attendance for poor and working-class students who are known to be loan adverse (Goldrick-Rab, 2016; Heller, 2013; McDonough, 1997). Sacks (2007) shares that poor and working-class students are "scared to death of the debt" and that fear is impacting their access to and enrollment in higher education (p. 176). Regardless of rural students' feelings, loans are now the most common way to finance higher education in the United States, with nearly 66% of all undergraduates taking out student loans (Goldrick-Rab, 2016).

Scholars and some policymakers are calling for a simplification of the student financial aid process and more assistance from high schools, colleges, and universities for rural, working-class families (McDonough et al., 2010). Suggestions include but are not limited to increasing assistance with completion of the FAFSA and other financial aid processes, reduction of the process complexity, providing more tailored information to specific family circumstances, and increasing transparency about criteria and award amounts (Goldrick-Rab, 2016; McDonough et al., 2010; Perna and Kurban, 2013).

College Knowledge

To add to application, admissions, and financial aid concerns, rural students also have to contend with social factors that influence their college access, including their college knowledge (Heller, 2013; Perna, 2013). Jones (2013) emphasizes the need to create and implement new strategies for "reaching out to, informing, and supporting students and families" (p. 4) and Perna (2013) recognizes "knowledge and information about college and financial aid" as one of the four most significant predictors of college enrollment (p. 15).

Relationship between College Knowledge and College Access

Research conducted by Vargas (2004) on behalf of The Education Resources Institute (TERI) found three relationships between college knowledge and students' educational aspirations (see Table 2.1). These findings express the importance of college knowledge and link it to higher education opportunities. Lack of information can be detrimental to rural students' college planning. Chenoweth and Galliher (2004) found college knowledge to be one of "the most important problems in rural students' college decision process" (p. 13). Students' college planning behavior will be shaped not only by information

Table 2.1. Relationships between College Knowledge and Educational Aspirations (Vargas, 2004, p. 3)

Relationship 1	College-preparatory information and guidance are major components in realizing college aspirations.
Relationship 2	Students typically underrepresented in higher education do not naturally possess college knowledge. Most come from families with limited or no college experience and attend schools that provide only minimal college guidance.
Relationship 3	The knowledge gap for underrepresented students is exacerbated by their limited access to technology and technological innovations in college admissions and recruitment via the Internet.

they have but also by the information and expectations they do not receive from their parents and high schools (Ganss, 2016; McDonough, 1997).

Obtaining the necessary higher education information is the most difficult for the students who need it the most—rural students—due to geographical and regional isolation that can limit accessibility to college knowledge (Chenoweth & Galliher, 2004). Rural students' struggles with college knowledge are rooted in their parents' inexperience with college, their schools' extremely limited guidance counselor staffing, and assumptions about students' prior, or inherent, college knowledge. Rural students' parents and schools can generally support the idea of college but often cannot provide the access to specific information or contacts that more privileged parents and schools can offer, nor can rural parents share firsthand experience of the benefits of higher education (Chenoweth & Galliher, 2004; Dumais & Ward, 2009; Ganss, 2016; Sacks, 2007). The National Center for Educational Statistics (NCES) (2013) reported that public schools have an average student-to-counselor ratio of 500:1, which represents the difficulty of seeking time-intensive help from school counselors. Schools and scholars continue to call for the hiring of additional counselors who could focus on providing rural students with the college knowledge needed to turn educational aspirations into realities and address transitions challenges (Bickel et al., 1991; Paulsen & Loflink, 2005).

Interventions to Equip Students with College Knowledge

Since rural, public high schools face resource and cultural limitations, university, community, state, and federal college access programs have been developed to provide rural students with college knowledge (e.g., TRIO programs, College Advising Corps, Bottom Line, and College Summit). White (2005) explored such a program in the University of Colorado at Boulder's Student Academic Services Center (SASC). The study's findings illustrated that students are not familiar with the linguistics styles or discourse used at the university nor its operational structure and how to work within that system, both of which resulted in confidence issues for students. Participants feared that their peers would judge them for their lack of "college talk" and "big words" (White, 2005, p. 385) and they struggled with GPA calculations, knowing where to get financial aid information, and understanding of the university registration system. The SASC was created to teach students the linguistic and navigational capital (Yosso, 2005) of the institution and students' engagement with UC-Boulder's program was shown to increase feelings of integrated into the university community and more confidence in language use.

Comparable to the UC-Boulder program, PK-12 and higher education systems in California collaborated to establish the "College Options" clearinghouse for rural California students. The clearinghouse attempts to "create college cultures, better prepare students academically, increase direct enrollment in four-year postsecondary schools, increase transfer rates from two-year to four-year institutions, raise family and community awareness of college options, and build infrastructure support for college and financial aid applications" (McDonough et al., 2010, p. 200). A similar early intervention college knowledge program for first-generation college students from Appalachia taught college "terminology," specifically concepts such as credit hours and section numbers and created a "safe reference place" for students to increase their understanding of college language and knowledge (Bryan & Simmons, 2009, p. 403). These are just a few examples of intervention strategies to help rural students gain college knowledge.

However, these programs often fight an uphill battle because intervention is needed earlier in the educational process—even as early as elementary school—to increase college access for rural populations (Flora et al., 2016; McDonough et al., 2010). Organization such as the National College Access Network (NCAN) work to build early interventions and teach college knowledge, but the consortium's community-based college access centers are typically in urban areas such as Philadelphia and Boston (Vargas, 2004). Therefore, rural students would have to travel to the largest cities in the state to reach a center, if they had access to NCAN's resources at all; states such as Delaware, Hawaii, Idaho, and Wyoming have no NCAN centers (NCAN member directory, 2010). While NCAN is just one example of a non-profit organization that is focused on college access, it highlights the pattern of resource differentiation between urban areas and rural areas. With fewer non-profit resources in rural areas, rural students often resort to acquiring college access information on their own.

Because of regional and resource constraints, McDonough et al. (2010) suggest two models to assist rural students in their acquisition of college knowledge, the first calling for a "university presence in every high school" in the country and the second calling for creation of a "community outreach center or hub" that would collaborate with high schools to provide information and support for "college preparation, planning, and culture" (p. 198). Both models require collaboration and commitment between PK-12 schools, higher education, and rural communities.

CONCLUSION

Rural students often do not have the same access to educational opportunities as their peers in suburban and urban areas. Varying family and school resources, proximity to higher education institutions, university recruiting and admissions practices, financial aid availability, and differing amounts of college knowledge are among the constraints rural students face. These challenges influence rural students' college predisposition, search, and choice and contribute to the stratification of higher education opportunity based on geography and social class. Further attention to how a college choice model and cultural capital frame rural students' experience with college access is provided in chapter 3.

Chapter 3

Putting the Pieces Together

Connections between a College Choice Model, Cultural Capital, and College Access, Knowledge, and Jargon

Interest in college access and choice is rooted in many U.S. families, educators, and policymakers viewing higher education as an essential element to personal success and social class mobility (Hossler & Palmer, 2012). The quality of high schools is increasingly being evaluated by the number of their students who have matriculated into colleges and universities (Hossler & Palmer, 2012), making college access not only an individual concern but also an institutional and societal one—a combination of the private good and the public good. Although rurality is seldom used as a higher education research lens, overarching college access and choice literature can provide a framework for understanding how college access is experienced by rural students.

College choice models combine economic, psychological, and sociological approaches to create developmental, multistage frameworks to describe how students' background and family circumstances, socialization, school experiences and opportunities, and academic abilities can influence college aspirations, access, and attendance (Hossler & Gallagher, 1987; Hossler & Palmer, 2012). Hossler and Palmer (2012) mention noteworthy historical models of college choice in Table 3.1.

HOSSLER AND GALLAGHER'S COLLEGE CHOICE MODEL

Hossler and Gallagher's (1987) three-phase college choice model is one of the most widely used college choice models and served as the theoretical framework for the case study of MapDot and its public high school. The model aligned with the study's purpose of exploring college access and choice through the specific lens of college knowledge and university jargon.

Table 3.1   Historical College Choice Models

Authors	Components of the College Choice Model
Chapman (1981)	• Search • Choice
Hanson and Litten (1982)	• Deciding to go to college • Investigating colleges • Application, admission, and attendance
Kotler and Fox (1985)	• Generic alternatives (college, work, military) • Product form alternatives (private or public) • Total college set • Awareness of set • Consideration of set • Choice set • Decision
Jackson (1986)	• Preference • Exclusion • Evaluation
Hossler and Gallagher (1987)	• Predisposition • Search • Choice

Hossler and Gallagher's (1987) developmental model considers how both individual and organizational factors influence college outcomes. The model contains three tiered stages—predisposition, search, and choice. The predisposition stage focuses on students' higher education aspirations, the search stage concentrates on students' access and institutional options, and the choice stage centers on where students commit to attend. The entire model, including its factors and outcomes, can be seen in Table 3.2.

The predisposition and search stages of Hossler and Gallagher's (1987) model were most relevant to understanding how rural students obtain college knowledge and decode university jargon. Rural students' predisposition was related to both individual and organizational factors including their academic aptitude, their high school's academic rigor and extracurricular options, the socioeconomic status and social class of their family and community, their parents' and peers' attitudes and encouragement toward college, and their proximity to a college campus (Hossler & Gallagher, 1987). These factors are some of the reasons rural students are often less likely to be predisposed to higher education aspirations. A summary of the predisposition phase can be found in Figure 3.1.

Many rural students stagnate in the predisposition stage and move out of the model to pursue other post–high school pathways, such as military service, technological training, or employment; however, a few rural students do move on to the search stage. Hossler and Gallagher's (1987) search stage concentrates on students' processes for seeking information about higher education options and includes interactions students may have with higher education institutions. Rural students' values and resources shape the questions they have and the information they obtain about colleges and universities. During the search stage, rural students should explore the differences between institutional types, costs, and offerings; however, accurate information can be difficult to find because of higher education marketing and recruiting practices. Institutions may embellish their offerings and services, use college knowledge without explaining it, or avoid recruiting in rural areas at all. In addition, rural students who are from working-class backgrounds and whose parents have less formal education tend to have longer and less efficient searches and seek more assistance from their high school counselors

Table 3.2   Hossler and Gallagher's (1987) Three Phase College Choice Model

Model Dimensions, or Phases	Individual Factors	Organizational Factors	Student Outcomes
Phase 1: Predisposition	• Student characteristics • Significant others • Educational activities	• School characteristics	• College options • Other post-high school options
Phase 2: Search	• Student preliminary college values • Student search activities	• College and university recruitment, marketing, and admissions activities	• College choice set • Other post-high school options set
Phase 3: Choice	• Choice set	• College and university "courtship" activities	• Choice

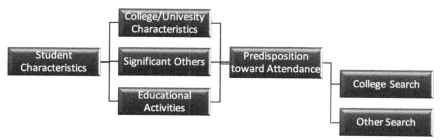

Figure 3.1   Summary of Hossler & Gallagher (1987) college choice model, stage one—predisposition. Adapted from original.

Figure 3.2 Summary of Hossler & Gallagher (1987) college choice model, stage two—search. Adapted from original.

(Hossler & Gallagher, 1987). Thus, rural students' search phase can often be impeded by lack of, or inaccurate, information about higher education options. A summary of the search phase can be found in Figure 3.2.

Hossler and Gallagher's (1987) model, particularly the predisposition and search stages, highlights how rural students often have more difficulty moving through the three stages of college choice because of both individual and organizational factors. This model also supports the relevance of studying college knowledge. If rural, public high school students neither possess knowledge about college or its jargon nor have the resources to obtain that knowledge, they may struggle with or be stunted in the predisposition and search stages of Hossler and Gallagher's (1987) model, which would limit the final stage of choice or reduce its likelihood altogether. Consequently, it is important to consider how rural students can bolster their college knowledge through various forms of capital.

BOURDIEU'S FORMS OF CAPITAL

Scholars frame social class identity as a composition of multiple forms of capital—financial, cultural, social, academic, linguistic, and navigational, to name a few (Bourdieu, 1986; Soria, 2015; Yosso, 2005). Bourdieu is one of the formative scholars on defining social class as capitals and his concepts inform educational and sociological research on the relationship between social class status and educational achievement (Archer, Hutchings, & Ross, 2003; MacLeod, 2009; McDonough, 1997; Mullen, 2010; Soria, 2015; Stuber, 2011). Bourdieu recognizes that educational systems favor those with privileged identities whose knowledge and behaviors are perceived as highly valuable and who have tools to navigate the systems, creating a social reproduction cycle, and he offers development of cultural and social capital as a means to interrupt this cycle (Mullen, 2010; Soria, 2015). The MapDot case study gives particular attention to cultural capital and how it shapes both individual and organizational college-going habitus in the rural, working-class community.

Cultural Capital

Bourdieu (1977) defines cultural capital as the knowledge, language, and culture that privileged families transmit to their children, such as valuing a college education for holistic development and economic security (Archer, 2003a; MacLeod, 2009; McDonough, 1997). The acquisition of cultural capital begins at home and involves cultural reproduction (Barratt, 2011; MacLeod, 2009; Schwalbe et al., 2000), which embraces the culture and practices of the dominant group as proper and normative, while coercing marginalized populations to "accept [their] place within existing hierarchies of status, power, and wealth" (Schwalbe et al., 2000, p. 429). So, while everyone possesses their own versions of cultural capital, educational institutions—including colleges and universities—tend to place the highest value on the cultural capital of the White, middle and upper classes who have collegiate experience (McDonough, 1997; Schwalbe et al., 2000; Soria, 2015).

Bourdieu (1977) describes individual cultural capital through two forms—static cultural capital and relational cultural capital. *Static cultural capital* represents a family's social class advantage through leisure choices, often referred to as "highbrow" cultural activities (e.g., plays, art galleries, museums) (Tramonte & Willms, 2009). *Relational cultural capital* describes the interactions and communication between children and parents, which influences how children relate with others (Bourdieu, 1977). Together, static and relational cultural capital molds students' approaches to relationship development and their tastes in hobbies.

Parents who possess more normative static and relational cultural capital expose their children to people, places, events, and situations to cultivate additional cultural capital and, thus, better prepare the children for experiences in educational institutions (Mullen, 2010; Schwalbe et al., 2000). Conversely, parents from marginalized identities often do not have the time, financial capital, or network capability to devote to cultural capital acquisition; they tend to assume their children will develop what they need in a natural way, which can potentially place their children at a disadvantage in educational institutions (McDonough et al., 2010; Mullen, 2010). Additionally, parents share cultural capital with their children about the value, process, and economic opportunities of education; parents' beliefs about education has been found to influence rural students' educational aspirations and attainment more than either aptitude or finances (Jencks, 1972). Cultural capital has also been found to have the largest effect on the quality of one's chosen higher education institution (McDonough, 1997). Thus, cultural capital impacts each stage of Hossler and Gallagher's (1987) model—college predisposition, search, and choice.

In addition to the individual cultural capital transmitted through families, rural schools impart organizational cultural capital and, subsequently, play a role in shaping rural students' cultural capital and educational aspirations (Schwalbe et al., 2000; Tramonte & Willms, 2009). From the organizational frame, cultural capital includes *embodied cultural capital*, or socialization practices; *objectified cultural capital*, or appreciation for "highbrow" activities and material possessions (i.e., static cultural capital); and *institutionalized cultural capital*, or credentials that confer status such as college degrees (Bourdieu, 1986; Dumais & Ward, 2009; Soria, 2015; Stuber, 2011).

Habitus

Cultural capital is further explained through the concept of habitus. *Habitus* is a deeply internalized, common set of viewpoints and experiences that individuals attain from their immediate environment (Bourdieu, 1977 & 1984; McDonough, 1997; McDonough et al., 2010). Habitus materializes as individuals' aspirations, perceptions, thoughts, feelings, expectations, practices, actions, and appreciations—an enduring sense of "one's place" in the world (Bourdieu, 1977; MacLeod, 2009; Mullen, 2010; Soria, 2015; Stuber, 2011). Often, rural students observe their family, school, and hometown habitus and then replicate it. The habitus that rural, first-generation, working-class folks share places a higher value on post–high school employment than on higher education (Corbett, 2007; Flora et al., 2016; McDonough et al., 2010; Willis, 1977), which is typically viewed as something for "others" but not something for "[rural] people like us" (Corbett, 2007, p. 3; Flora et al., 1992). This viewpoint is illustrated by a participant in Willis' (1977) study who noted that "an ounce of keenness is worth a whole library of certificates" (p. 56).

Like cultural capital, habitus can be viewed from both the individual perspective and the organizational perspective. *Organizational habitus* is the high school or community's additional impact on students' belief system and behavior, including college-going (McDonough, 1997; Perna & Kurban, 2013). Organizational habitus exhibits the mutually shaping relationship between high schools' organizational culture and the community's social class and demonstrates how the habitus informs rural students' perceptions of higher education (Corbett, 2007; McDonough, 1997). Individuals within the high school—counselors, teachers, and administrators—and within the community influence rural students' access to college knowledge resources and opportunities (Perna & Kurban, 2013).

Because of their habitus, privileged students see college as a place where they belong, while rural, working-class, and first-generation college students do not have a natural inclination for college or full understanding of its admission process and, thus, often choose to forgo a college education (Dumais & Ward, 2009). McDonough et al. (2010) affirm that "college is outside the habitus of many rural students" (p. 203).

Significance of Cultural Capital and Habitus to College Access

Social mobility and economic prospects are tied to educational opportunity; education and social class are two of the variables used to explain U.S. cultural and regional divides and are closely connected to cultural capital (Kim & Kim, 2009). Rural students do not naturally inherit the cultural capital that is necessary to seek out or be successful in higher education (McDonough, 1997; Soria, 2015) because of families' inexperience or unfamiliarity with college processes. Dumais and Ward (2009) found that family cultural capital, cultural classes, and parental involvement in the college admissions process were all significant to rural students' enrollment and persistence.

Additionally, rural students often possess a "community-fostered way of knowing and understanding that is at odds with the literacies imperative for university success" (Whiting, 1999, p. 158). What rural students know is often different from what is needed to fit into the higher education culture; thus, rural students feel unprepared for and unwelcome in the collegiate environment (O'Quinn, 1999; Whiting, 1999; Soria, 2015). Even when rural students possess college knowledge and achieve academic success, they often find themselves on the periphery, never being fully accepted into academia because their cultural capital is recently acquired rather than naturally derived from their home environments (Corbett, 2007; Schafft & Jackson, 2010; Soria, 2015). Further exacerbating the issue, rural students' development of cultural capital is limited by the cultural capital that they bring into higher education with them (Schwalbe et al., 2000).

High schools, colleges, and universities often fail at bridging this cultural capital divide between privileged and marginalized students. In fact, structural analyses reveal that educational institutions actually sort people into certain academic areas and occupations by identity groups to retain wealth, power, and influence with those who already have it—the White, middle and upper class—and, thus, perpetuate inequities (Aronson, 2008; Barratt, 2011; MacLeod, 2009; McDonough et al., 2010). Rural students are often evaluated by normative definitions and standards that view their forms of knowledge and capital as deficient (Flora et al., 1992; MacLeod, 2009). Known as the concept of "othering," this practice identifies a dominant group and an inferior group and is "aimed at creating and/or reproducing inequality" and defining "difference as deficient" (Schwalbe et al., 2000, p. 422–423). There is a push and pull in all levels of education, including higher education, between those who support the status quo and its process of "othering" and those who strive for social justice.

Academic Discourse and Cultural Capital

Language and communication practices are some of the most active and elusive parts of a person's cultural heritage and background, making it difficult for educational institutions to break their social reproduction of cultural capital and habitus because these institutions contain linguistic and cultural competencies that convey the White, middle- and upper-class culture (Bourdieu 1965; Bourdieu, 1977). Academia has unique discourses that emphasize privileged cultural capitals of language and communication.

Discourse is a socially accepted way people use language, thought, and behavior to align with a specific identity group, or groups, and express their power (Schwalbe et al., 2000). Gee (1998) considers discourses to be inherently ideological and, subsequently, exclusionary toward marginalized groups because privileged discourses often increase acquisition of social goods such as money, power, and status in a society. There are *primary discourses* that people acquire through families and *secondary discourses* that are taught in institutions, such as schools (Gee, 1998). Secondary discourses may be misaligned with the primary discourses; for example, how someone learns to talk at home can often differ from how one is expected to talk at school. Rural students often possess low-prestige discourses—word choices, accents, etc.—and others may try to prove power and status over them by using exclusionary language or jargon (Barratt, 2011; Gee, 1998).

Discourses can be powerful tools for social reproduction because they can normalize thought and emotion, create a system of "othering," and perform boundary maintenance (Schwalbe et al., 2000). As such, rural students may feel forced to adopt the normed discourse of higher education (e.g., academic language and university jargon) in order to aspire to or access college. Bourdieu (1965) called academic language "a dead language and no one's mother tongue, not even that of . . . the cultivated classes" (p. 8). The difference between the language of the family and community and the language of the school creates a barrier and sense of exclusion among students—especially rural, working-class, first-generation college students—and an assumption that the education system is an elite environment.

Cultural Capital and Cultural Transition of Rural Students

While there is often a significant cultural transition for all students who enter higher education, rural students' transition can sometimes be more difficult because of their unfamiliarity with the culture, habitus, and discourse in academia and academia's lack of value in rural students' existing capital and culture. Changes in culture—such as the transition to college—often require changes in language use (O'Quinn, 1999; White, 2005; Whiting, 1999; Zwerling & London, 1992).

White's (2005) study provided accounts of students feeling like outsiders at their institutions, attributable to their lack of college knowledge. One student noted that he did not talk like his peers and worried that they would judge him based on his language, while another student attributed her academic difficulties to differences in language use and a lack of understanding of the university system (White, 2005). Contrasts in income, social styles, and language use may cause many rural students to feel like outsiders in higher education, forcing them to either learn a new culture and kind of vocabulary or remain on the periphery (Cushman, 2007; Dumais & Ward, 2009).

Rural students are often challenged to remain true to themselves in an environment where they feel "othered" and struggle with the cultural conflicts between their new college-oriented world and the world of their hometown friends, families, and rural communities (Martin, 2015). Kempner (1991) defined *cultural conflicts* as a situation in which one's own beliefs, values, and symbols clash with normed behaviors. Rural students must negotiate between their different sociocultural worlds and find a balance between their multiple identities and multiple environments (McDonough, 1997; Whiting, 1999; Zwerling & London, 1992). Some students continually move in and out of different cultures (Cushman, 2007); for example, students in White's (2005) study discussed their tendency to shift their language based on context and audience, using certain words in their home community and others in the university community. Similarly, in Simmons and Bryan's (2009) study of family involvement and impact on first-generation Appalachian college students, participants expressed feelings of being two separate people—one at home and one at school—which creates a cultural tension for rural students trying to fit in with both the higher education environment and their home environment.

Cultural Capital, College Knowledge, and University Jargon

Higher education institutions have their own culture and social context and rural students are challenged to find meaning and values in this unfamiliar setting (Ganss, 2016; Whiting, 1999). As part of their culture, colleges and universities have specific institutional jargon as part of their academic discourse. Rural students likely do not know this jargon, which can lead to feelings of inadequacy and alienation from the collegiate environment (White, 2005). This jargon is an aspect of the broader college knowledge that often creates misalignment between rural students' cultural capital and that of academia

(Whiting, 1999). Even though the college knowledge gap is severe, Vargas (2004) suggests that it is not impossible to overcome, and he proposes policies for college access that focus on ways to provide marginalized students with the information and guidance they need—both early and often. Scholars recommend that college advising focus on resources for students and families with the least knowledge of the system, those who need extra support in the college choice process—choosing colleges, applying, and getting financial aid (Cushman, 2007; Hossler & Gallagher, 1987).

Bourdieu's (1965 & 1977) concepts of cultural capital and habitus can be used as a framework for exploring rural students' ability to access college, particularly in reference to college knowledge and university jargon. The interaction of these concepts—cultural capital and habitus, academic discourse, and college knowledge and university jargon—is a dynamic process. Ideally, building on rural students' existing cultural capital and habitus will assist them in learning academic discourse and college knowledge and developing skills to decode university jargon. This process can increase rural, working-class, first-generation college students' access to and success within college.

CONCLUSION

Hossler and Gallagher's (1987) College Choice Model and Bourdieu's (1965 & 1977) concepts of cultural capital and habitus layer together to provide a framework for exploring how rural students' cultural capital impacts their college aspirations and access—their predisposition, search, and choice. Building upon rural students' existing cultural capital and reframing their habitus will enable them to better comprehend college knowledge and decode university jargon, which could increase their access to college.

However, we cannot nurture rural students' ability to decode university jargon without insight into their individual and organizational cultural capital and habitus, their educational aspirations, and the processes and resources they currently use to acquire college knowledge and decode university jargon. Chapters 4 and 5 focus on these topics through the experiences of Taylor, Landry, and Ms. Guillory at MapDot High School.

Chapter 4

"More Trouble Than It's Worth or a Path to a 'Better Life'?"

Rural Attitudes About College

As chapter 3 demonstrated, cultural capital and habitus can be major guiding forces in how individuals and communities view and value educational opportunities. MapDot's students, public high schools, and community provided insight into how cultural capital and habitus can be influential in rural students' views of and aspirations to higher education.

The rural county in which MapDot High School is located reports that only 68% of the population has a high school diploma and 12% have a bachelor's degree, in contrast to national averages of 86% and 29%, respectively (U.S. Census, 2015). These statistics suggest that MapDot residents may have static and relational cultural capital and individual and organizational habitus that steer students away from formal, postsecondary education because it is not viewed as a realistic option for most people in MapDot. The data also implies that many people in the area engage in careers or jobs that do not require much formal, postsecondary education and typically have lower incomes or longer workdays.

Taylor, Landry, and Ms. Guillory—representatives of MapDot and its public high school—provide insight into the local belief systems; financial climate; opportunities for exposure to other ways of thinking or being; occupation examples and role models; and any advantages or resources available to MapDot High School's students.

MAPDOT'S BELIEF SYSTEM

MapDot's community habitus aligns with common rural belief systems that influence individuals' habitus. People's principles and life paths are influenced by similar community sentiments on the value of education and the desire to remain isolated from "other" (e.g., suburban and urban) ways of thinking and being. The public high schools' cultures reflect the broader community habitus and social class culture, all of which "shape students' perceptions of appropriate college choices, thereby affecting patterns of educational attainment" (McDonough, 1997, p. 153). Essentially, rural students' plans and goals tend reflect their family and community values and influences (McDonough, 1997); MapDot and its public high school illustrate this cultural process.

Views on Educational Value

The value of higher education opportunities ranges from community members who believe a formal education is essential to those who think formal education is a complete waste of time because it takes time away from working and making money. With over 30% of residents without high school diplomas and 88% with no college experience, the feelings about higher education span from encouraging to antagonistic. To many of these rural residents, education is "more trouble than it's worth." Ms. Guillory, MapDot High's counselor, explained:

> We still have a lot of kids who are the first people in their family to graduate high school. Education in a lot of the families is not a priority. In some, [education is], but for a lot, it's not . . . a lot of the kids do go straight to work. We have many parents that don't value education at all and won't sacrifice to help their kids get to school. And then we also have some that really do and really push their kids. At [MapDot High], I would say the majority [of parents and students] don't value education as much as they should.

If parents, other family members, or community leaders did not care about education, students seemed less likely to have academic success or desire to pursue further education. Alternatively, if people significant to them supported education, students seemed more motivated to strive for academic achievement and aspirations. Landry, a student at MapDot High, described how some students at MapDot High could care less about education while others did care, a contrast which he believed mirrored adults in the community. He also shared about the culture of dropping out at MapDot High School. Taylor, another student, spoke more about the positive messages from the community about trying to go to college to create a "better life," a commonly used phrase in MapDot that highlighted the unrealized educational aspirations of community members who hoped for "something more" but did not get to achieve it.

There were also wide-ranging viewpoints on the importance of school, or "book," knowledge and practical, or hands-on, knowledge in MapDot. Most

MapDot High students believed that an individual should cultivate a combination of academic and applied knowledge to lead a balanced career and life. The rural students associated school/book knowledge with being "smart" and practical/hands-on knowledge with having "common sense." Landry explained this philosophy as the importance of being able to both know things *and* actually do things.

Converse to the students' claim to value both types of knowledge equally, their public high school counselor, Ms. Guillory, believed that the majority of MapDot High School students tended to gravitate toward practical knowledge. She said she could understand why students may place more value in practical/hands-on knowledge and gave examples about how she had seen practical knowledge be rewarded more in the county and in her own family, where skill-based jobs are more prevalent and, sometimes, more prosperous. The varying community perspectives on education and the value of "head work versus hand work" often left MapDot High students with mixed messages about whether or not the pursuit of a college education was worthwhile.

While rural students may receive some positive encouragement from parents and family members, they are also subject to the negative attitudes from other parents and community members. Taylor explained how she receives messages from folks in MapDot that college is not for everybody, but that her parents told her she should always want to "better" herself and she still held on to the belief that higher education might be for her. Rural students often associated the positive value of college with economic returns or "easier," "white collar" work that they assumed came with a college degree. Landry expressed that education was a good thing because it made it easier to get a job and kept you from having to "work hard your whole life." Ms. Guillory also heard clashing messages about higher education from the MapDot community. She described how some parents thought all students should go to college, while others pushed their students to go directly into the workforce, with a few even encouraging students to drop out of high school to expedite the process to employment.

Despite the positive outcomes that Taylor and Landry connected with college, the rural students characterized higher education as something often reserved for only the elite. Students suggested that "people like them" do not often enroll in or graduate from college. Taylor described how not everybody can go to college because of hurdles like completing high school, which they knew and saw did not happen for everyone in MapDot. The rural students were also cognizant that people who did attend and/or graduate from college often had to deal with the community viewing them as elite or "too good" for their home area. A college education often resulted in rural students not being able to find jobs in MapDot, or the broader county, because the majority of local jobs did not require higher education. Additionally, college was seen by the community as a place that opens up the mind to new, or different, ideas and ways of being that could conflict with the way of life in the rural area. In short, being college-educated often educated students out of their home community, both literally and figuratively.

Peer Groups

Despite the community's habitus and viewpoints, students perceived educational aspirations among their peers. They discussed how most of their peers planned on going to college and how some students even intended to go to the same institutions and become roommates. However, they also mentioned perceived ambivalence among their peers when it came to clarifying post–high school plans. Taylor explained how some of her friends wished to pursue college, others were targeting technical schools, and a few were not going to go anywhere. Landry was even more specific, stating that half of his friends wanted to go to college and the other half want to go straight to the oil field and make money.

OCCUPATIONAL PATHS

Cultural capital is often reflected through the community's common jobs or careers—and their corresponding salaries and benefits—as well as people's access to potential role models. MapDot High School's students often looked to their community to figure out what was considered a good job or good life and, subsequently, based their future plans off of these observations.

Students, teachers, and administrators at MapDot High School acknowledged that the majority of residents in the rural county were employed in particular occupational fields. Typical job paths included but are not exclusively limited to the oil field; medical field—primarily nursing, x-ray tech, and respiratory tech; small, local business; factory work, such as the Wal-Mart distribution center in the neighboring county; clerical work; law enforcement; PK-12 education; and other manual or skilled labor fields such as farming, welding, pipelining, and cosmetology. Residents often classified their jobs as "blue collar" because the jobs involve more manual labor, higher risks, lower incomes, and less necessary training or education. Ms. Guillory noted the dominance of the oil field, the decline of local hospital jobs because of budget cuts, and the dependence on service-based jobs at businesses such as Wal-Mart, Piggly Wiggly, and the dollar stores.

MapDot High School students were clear about the jobs that "everybody does around here." It was very obvious that the rural students understood where the jobs were in their community and who got to do which ones. They were inclined to label fields by sex, noting what they felt were the female designated careers—nursing/medical field and K-12 education—and the male designated careers—oil field, manual labor, or small, local business. Taylor spoke about how she saw most women choose jobs in the medical or PK-12 education fields, while Landry shared how he felt compelled to go into "men's jobs" like the oil field.

"Brain Drain"

When individuals are seeking a career or higher education outside of the typical occupational paths described above, it often means they will have to leave the community—potentially forever. This is known as "brain drain"—when young, talented, and intelligent individuals departing their community for better education and job opportunities elsewhere (Corbett, 2007; Theobald & Siskar, 2008). Brain drain is one of the main issues for rural communities, including MapDot (Carr & Kefalas, 2009). Taylor could already see this happening as she looked into her future: "[Success] is me getting out of here, you know, just not staying here. There's nothing for me here besides family and friends, but I want to see the world and do all that I can." Rural students often saw their community as limiting and isolating, and they knew that many careers requiring a college education would ultimately educate them out of the occupational choices in MapDot. Some students sounded hopeful and excited about the idea of leaving the rural community, while others had a hint of regret about seeking the type of success that would result in having to depart their home.

Role Models

Because of the restricted occupational choices in MapDot and its surrounding county, and the impact of brain drain, rural students are often constrained in their knowledge about potential career paths. It is tough to imagine a job or career you have neither heard of nor seen, although a few students like Taylor did have aspirations of doing "something different." This sparks a new challenge for the rural students to find "someone like them" who has blazed the trail in a different occupation and can answer questions or serve as a mentor. Ms. Guillory explained how MapDot High School educators try to use their personal contacts to provide students with a role model in the field to which they aspire; she acknowledged:

> Well, there's very few [role models]. There's not a lot of job opportunities here, especially this little town. But, I have a senior this year that wants to be a veterinarian, so I called and spoke to a friend of mine that's a vet and set up

for her to do some volunteer work there. [If] people are interested in pharmacy or engineering or attorney, I try to think of someone I know personally and say, "Hey, would you mind talking to this kid? Is it okay if they call you or do some job shadowing or something like that?" We don't have a permanent thing set in place, but I do something like that, even if it's just a telephone conversation.

While there may be limitations, educators tried to do their best to utilize MapDot's "everyone knows everyone" outlook to find a few role models for students interested in occupational paths considered "out of the box" for the rural area.

FINANCIAL CLIMATE

Because of the typical occupations in MapDot, residents are often members of the poor and working classes. The median household income in the county is $30,232, compared to a national average of $53,482, with 24% of people falling below the poverty line (U.S. Census, 2015). Approximately 80% of the students in MapDot county's public schools participate in the Federal Free or Reduced Lunch Program, which further illustrates the financial situation in the county (State Department of Education, 2011). Students recognized that they resided in a poor and working-class area; Taylor bluntly stated: "I mean, nobody's rich. Nobody has a lot of money around here. But it depends on [what family] you're from . . . I guess."

Since their families tend to have modest incomes, many rural students already worked. They served in part-time capacities as babysitters, clerks in local stores, and in manual labor roles to have spending money, participate in school activities, and finance their technology and transportation. Ms. Guillory explained that many students were tasked with financing their own transportation—buying used cars, paying for insurance and gas, etc.—and paying their cell phone bills. Rural students had to work in order to have those conveniences.

The students and Ms. Guillory also mentioned the impact of the regional and national economy on the rural community. A reduction in jobs and services at the local hospital and rumors that the hospital might close permanently had many individuals and families concerned about their personal finances and the well-being of the community at large. Landry even talked about how his brother had to drop out of college because "the economy is so bad . . . he decided to go offshore [in the oil field]." And, each time the price of oil dropped and layoffs hit the petroleum industry, MapDot's economy was heavily impacted. The students frequently saw their families and community members struggling and they recognized that one way to potentially improve their own futures was to further their formal education.

What the students did not mention, contrary to the literature, were expectations that they forgo college to contribute to family finances, which is often seen in poor and working-class urban communities and within Hispanic/Latinx families. The rural students that go straight to work—in the oil field, for example—do so to make their own money and support their own lifestyle, rather than to contribute to the family's income. There is not an overarching community expectation that kids will financially assist families, although there is a common practice of rural children caring for their aging parents. Students do not believe they have to leave the rural community to "survive" but there is a view that you have to leave to thrive—to lead a "better life."

EXPOSURE TO OR ISOLATION FROM "OTHER WAYS"

All of the rural students in the study were born and raised in MapDot county, or one that was strikingly similar and within a two-hour radius of MapDot High School, and their lives have remained relatively isolated to the region. Ms. Guillory shared that the rural nature of MapDot means students do not get a lot of exposure to people outside the area and many students have never left the state. The rural students who had some exposure to people, places, and ideas outside of MapDot did so for three main purposes—1) to attend an extracurricular activity, 2) to go on a family vacation, or 3) to visit family in other states. Unlike their more affluent peers, rural students did not travel to gain cultural or global perspectives. Even when students did get out of the state, they often remained in the southeastern region of the United States, which cultivated similar ways of thinking and being. Ms. Guillory recognized these patterns of trips focusing on family and sports (or other extracurricular activities), and students affirmed that their out-of-state travel focused on extracurricular activities in which they, or their family members, were engaged.

Ms. Guillory believed that students would benefit from additional exposure to other ways of being and thinking. She described how students could broaden their perspectives, learn from different cultures, and be exposed to new expectations from other areas of the United States or world. Particularly, she thought "it would be wonderful" if students could experience the emphasis other communities put on education—the aim to "not to be so simpleminded or [have] tunnel vision"—and gain more of Bourdieu's (1977) static cultural capital though "highbrow activities," including museums and the arts, which often represent social class advantage (Bourdieu, 1977; Tramonte & Willms, 2010). From conversations with both Ms. Guillory and the students, it seemed that MapDot High School students would benefit from further exposure to places outside of the state, people who did not share their identities, and activities that focused on culture, arts, and science—all of which would bolster their cultural capital.

EXTRACURRICULAR ADVANTAGES AND CHALLENGES

Similar to their exposure to outside perspectives and people, rural students also varied in their experience with extracurricular activities and hobbies. While some MapDot High School students were highly engaged in their school extracurricular activities—involvement often highlighted on college applications, other students chose to engage in hobbies that were perceived as less valuable or prestigious than those of their suburban or urban peers. Taylor described her inherent interest and enjoyment in reading and her membership on the school's cheerleading squad. She, along with Landry, was also highly involved with school and community athletic teams. Their extracurricular involvement choices were advantageous in several ways, including putting the rural students in positions to visit colleges—for experiences such as cheerleading and football camp—and be included on the prospective student lists for some university admissions offices.

Other interests did not align as well with college-going. Landry's hunting and fishing hobbies and after-school job did not necessarily parallel activities that universities desire or that give students access to cultural capital that is advantageous in college. In many cases, what rural students knew and enjoyed was different from higher education cultural norms; thus, students may feel unprepared for and unwelcome in the collegiate environment (O'Quinn, 1999; Whiting, 1999). The issue is that "by the definition and standards of the school [systems]," rural students are often evaluated through a deficit lens that does not give appropriate value to their forms of knowledge and capital (Flora et al., 1992; MacLeod, 2009, p. 101). Hobbies like hunting and fishing take patience and knowledge of nature; part-time jobs teach time management, customer service, and responsibility; and entertaining oneself in a remote area with little financial or community resources shows initiative, independence, and creativity. However, higher education often overlooks these knowledge-bases and skills that rural students exhibit.

MIXED SIGNALS ABOUT EDUCATIONAL CHOICES

Inequalities exist in rural schools' resources, their lack of "the right kind of students," and their inability to offer honors, advanced placement, and international baccalaureate courses (Jencks, 1972, p. 37; McDonough et al., 2010). Rural students often face challenges to their academic preparation

and higher education aspirations because of their social class, low educational attainment in their families, and a limited number of community
members with college degrees (Brown & Swanson, 2003). MapDot High
School students' beliefs about their life choices after high school were often
regulated by their academic aptitude, finances, and self-efficacy and support
systems.

Academic Aptitude

At the time of this study, MapDot High School did not offer any specialized programs or courses, such as international baccalaureate (IB) degrees
and advanced placement (AP) courses, and the state typically graded their
school performance in the C range (State Department of Education, 2011).
MapDot High tended to struggle with cultural, financial, and human capital
resources, although it had been faring a bit better since MapDot residents
passed a tax to renovate the school. The majority of MapDot High students
were average or below average in their academic aptitude, with graduation
rates hovering around 70% (County School Board, 2010). Approximately
80% of the MapDot students are also considered "at-risk" because of their
enrollment in the federal free/reduced lunch program (State Department of
Education, 2011).

Despite the statistics and even their personal academic credentials, Ms.
Guillory noted that many of the rural students believed they were going to
college, at least in the earlier years of high school. She explained that students' college aspirations started high but tended to wane throughout high
school because they were not well prepared, lacked good study habits, and
were frequently absent from school. Ms. Guillory believed students could be
unrealistic in their aspirations and did not understand the dedication that college required, particularly regarding study skills. She provided the example
of students who had 1.8 GPAs and low ACT scores, yet still talked about
becoming a doctor or veterinarian and how reality would eventually "slap
them in the face" because higher education was not academically feasible for
these students. "I mean, you've got to be really bright [to go to college]. Not
everybody is really bright. Even if I tell them or try to explain it to them over
and over again, it doesn't always sink in," Ms. Guillory explained. However,
she also remarked that some MapDot High School students were on target
academically to pursue higher education. While most students in the study
did not divulge their personal academic abilities or grades, Landry did admit
that his family kept pushing him to get better grades; he disclosed that grades
were one of his main challenges because his current GPA was not going to
get him into a "good college" so both he and his family knew he had to get
his "grades up."

Student Finances

Leaving MapDot, particularly to pursue higher education, is often a major financial issue for rural students. Ms. Guillory confirmed that money was the most prevalent barrier to college access because many parents did not have a high school diploma, much less a college degree, and could not afford to pay for students' higher education. In addition, she highlighted the additional college costs—room, board, and living expenses—as substantial obstacles for even the most academically capable MapDot High School students.

Financial issues were symbolized in an occurrence one afternoon in Ms. Guillory's office. Three students were at the computer stations trying to complete the application for the upcoming ACT test but could not do so because Ms. Guillory had run out of ACT fee waivers. The students were antsy to learn that fee waivers were currently unavailable because the deadline to register for the upcoming test was the following day and they could not afford to pay for the test fee themselves. Later that afternoon, additional fee waivers become available and, once the announcement was made over the intercom, students immediately rushed into Ms. Guillory's office and formed a line. It was obvious that the students' ability to take the ACT was contingent upon having access to fee waivers, which illustrates the impact finances can have on rural students' college aspirations and access. Ms. Guillory noted how students were both aware of and worried about the money it takes to pursue higher education. Taylor was one of several students who noted that "paying for college" would be a barrier for her, and Landry foresaw the challenge of simultaneously working and going to college and finding enough time for both.

Self-Efficacy and Support Systems

Wettersten et al. (2005) explain how barriers and social support impact rural adolescents' self-efficacy, outcome expectations, and vocational interests. Rural students' career expectations are influenced by their social support and self-efficacy, which represent the powerful role of relationships—particularly those between parents and children. Students at MapDot High School displayed some confidence in their ability to pursue higher education and motivation to overcome the barriers that might have obstructed their educational opportunities. However, the rural students did recognize that their path would not be easy because many "people like them" have struggled or failed in their own attempts to obtain an education.

Ms. Guillory highlighted how some students were really determined and just kept persevering toward college until they figured it out while others quit when they reached a certain frustration level. Rural students also tended to assume that their communities would prefer for them not to attend college because parents and peers did not offer overt support (James et al., 1999; O'Quinn, 1999). However, despite these concerns, the MapDot High School study participants believed their families were relatively supportive of their educational aspirations.

Family Concerns and Support

Leaving MapDot can be difficult for students who have grown up in such a tight-knit community surrounded by their immediate and extended families. The link between education and community departure is "for some students . . . liberating, for others unthinkable, and for most it is problematic and conflicted" (Corbett, 2007, p. 18). Landry explained how his five-year-old sister had health concerns that take up a lot of the family's time and finances and it would be both a personal and financial challenge for him to depart MapDot. Taylor shared how her family was not eager for her to go to college because they are anxious about her being a single woman in a "big city." Other students discussed how they planned to begin their educational pursuits at local community colleges close to MapDot.

Despite some concerns, the majority of MapDot High students felt they had adequate emotional support from their families about their educational choices. The rural students felt supported yet able to make choices about their future on their own terms. Landry shared:

> [My family] thinks I'm on the right track for my future. They think I'm doing the right things. They say I can do anything I want as long as I put my heart into it. They think I should [go to college], but if I don't want to and I want to go straight to work, they'd be all right with it.

Other MapDot High students felt forced by their parents or families to choose higher education. This could be viewed as either overwhelming support, a burden, or both. Ms. Guillory pointed out that some students confided in her that their parents were not giving them an option—they had to go to college. This was the case for Taylor, who described:

> I mean they want me to go of course. I mean, doesn't every parent? My dad and my mom don't even give me a choice. I have to go to college because my dad didn't go to college. And my mom had trouble too [because she didn't go]. [They say life] will be easier once—like I get out of high school and just go straight to college. They say you need to go, it'll be good for you. You can do stuff we never got to do. That's what they want so I guess I'll do it.

Peer Influence

The choices and support of their peers can often influence rural students' educational and life choices as well. MapDot county has a history of teenage pregnancy and youth crime and students knew they faced critical choices that could complicate their pursuit of further education. Alternatively, Ms. Guillory noticed the positive persuasion MapDot High School students could have on one another; she explained how groups of students swayed each other, giving the example of the Class of 2013 who had much more interest in college because their friends were also showing interest. The shared motivation encouraged students to visit Ms. Guillory's office or complete their applications together. Whether or not rural students had family and peer support systems, they still sought support from their public high school counselor. This is both an endorsement of the counselors' work and a battle of competing interests, which will be discussed further in chapter 6.

STUDENTS' COLLEGE HOPES, DREAMS, AND REALITIES

While rural students are significantly underrepresented in higher education, at least half of all the students at MapDot High School and all of this study's participants intend to pursue some sort of postsecondary education—through a technical/trade school, community college, or four-year institution. They hoped that certificates and degrees would lead them to fulfilling careers, steady finances, and a "better life."

A Community College Mentality

Rural students who aspire to higher education often possess a "community college mentality," which means that many of them focus on community colleges rather than four-year institutions in order to remain in the community and ease into higher education (McDonough, Gildersleeve, & Jarsky, 2010, p. 199). Hu (2003) found that rural students sought a two-year education more than any other type of higher education and at rates higher than both their urban and suburban peers.

MapDot High School students were inclined to only consider higher education institutions that were a one- to two-hour drive from their town. The majority of the students focused on two local community colleges—branch campuses of the state flagship institution—as the most probable options for their institutional choice. One of these institutions is approximately a 25-minute drive from the county while the other institution is approximately a 45-minute drive from the county. Taylor explained that she might want to start her college experience close to home to "get up on my feet and then transfer to another school." Ms. Guillory recognized, and sometimes even encouraged, this community college mentality; she expected that most students would stay close to MapDot and attend one of the two community colleges that the students mentioned. She believed these institutions were good starting places, even though students who begin their higher education journey at community colleges often face additional retention and transfer challenges, particularly for those who have goals of obtaining a four-year degree.

Academic and Career Interests

Rural students participating in this study were at different points in the education and career decision-making processes. Some students could only name various subjects that were strengths or struggles for them, while others could articulate career fields that they intended to pursue. Taylor lacked clarity about her future career plans, and Landry was more focused on college as a means of leaving the area and continuing his participation in athletics, but he did have a backup plan of working in a technological field or as a physical therapist if professional athletics did not transpire for him. Other students seemed to align their career interests with the typical community habitus in MapDot, specifically focusing on the occupational fields of education, medical technicians, and agriculture and farming.

"Better Life" as Success

During discussions about their college aspirations, MapDot High students kept mentioning the same phrase to characterize why they planned to pursue a college education—they wanted to have a "better life." The phrase seemed to be a mantra that the students adopted from their families and from the community habitus. In almost every interview, the concept of a "better life," if not the exact phrase, arose.

Landry explained that he believed most people wanted to go to college to do better in life, which he defined as being able to "get a good job, meet the needs of your family, put food on the table, and live a good life without having to struggle." He believed that money was the driver of college aspirations because people in MapDot were always worried about money. Taylor shared that her parents and other MapDot community members wanted her to better herself through college and she wanted that too; a better life for Taylor meant "doing something" with her future. When asked about the "better life" concept, Ms. Guillory affirmed that it involved students obtaining more education than their parents in order to have more opportunities, but she added that it was about more than income alone. The "better life" was also about students finding a career that they enjoyed and made them happy—indulgences that many people in MapDot never got to experience.

Although this study focuses on cultural capital, it is important to note how human capital arose in this portion of the study data. Everyone's explanations of the "better life" concept—and the financial gain as success idea—supported investment in human capital. Paulsen (2001) describes *investment in human capital* as spending time and money on education and other activities to develop one's "knowledge, understandings, talents, and skills" (p. 56). Specifically, rural students' desire for a better life tied into the human capital notion that there would be multiple types of return on their investment in higher education (Paulsen, 2001). Students would decide to pursue higher education if, and only if, they believed "a college education is worthwhile," which meant that they would assume the future benefits of pursing a higher education would outweigh the present costs of attending (Paulsen, 2001, p. 56). However, human capital is not the sole determinant of students' decision to aspire to or attend college. Rather, factors that are directly explored in this study such as academic ability, social class identity, geography, and access to college knowledge information—and university jargon—also contribute to students' college decision-making.

Aspirations vs. Reality

Rural students' varying career aspirations and desire for a "better life" were not a surprise to their public high school counselor. Ms. Guillory had spent over 30 years in MapDot county listening to the dreams of public high school students. The issue she faced was helping students balance their aspirations with reality. She explained that, while some students aspired to college because it seemed fun or like a natural next step, others really had an educational goal in mind, although those goals were sometimes "far-fetched." She shared her own story of how she could have never gone into nursing because "blood and guts make her nauseous" and how she had to help students understand their capabilities and how to align their skill sets and preferences with career choices.

It was apparent that, during her formal and informal interactions with students, Ms. Guillory attempted to balance out aspirations and realities. One afternoon in her office, there was a discussion between two students about how they could never get into a school like Harvard. Ms. Guillory explained to the students that their priority of focus needed to be on passing their graduation exit exam, and they should remember what academic track they were on [Core 4 vs. Basic curriculum]. She also mentioned that the students should not worry about Harvard not wanting them because Harvard would not have wanted her either and there were plenty of other colleges and universities out there. The exchange between Ms. Guillory and the students showed both her encouragement of the students and her efforts to refocus them on more realistic, attainable goals.

CONCLUSION

Rural communities like MapDot and their people—represented by Taylor, Landry, and Ms. Guillory—have inconsistent attitudes about higher education. While the idea of higher education was usually supported in theory, the realities that higher education presented for rural students could be daunting. The white, middle- and upper-class norms of colleges and universities can be in opposition to the local, rural belief systems and result in apprehensions about rural students being changed and educated out of the occupational opportunities in their hometowns. There were also mixed signals about the actual choices rural students had for higher education because of financial constraints, academic opportunities, and support systems pushing and pulling them in conflicting directions. While it was clear that rural students have similar hopes and dreams as their suburban and urban peers, the path to realizing a "better life" for themselves was filled with complexities—one of which was acquiring college knowledge—which is addressed in chapter 5.

Chapter 5

"I Know What B.S. Means, Just Not in Those Terms"

Rural Students' Encounters with College Knowledge

One of the complexities that rural, working-class, first-generation college students have to navigate during their predisposition and search phases of Hossler and Gallagher's (1987) college choice model is developing college knowledge, including the specific language that is spoken in higher education—university jargon. Since colleges and universities often normalize white, middle- and upper-class cultural capital, college knowledge can be a barrier for rural students from poor and working-class backgrounds who will be the first in their families pursue higher education. This study found three steps that rural students can follow to build their college knowledge: 1) Becoming Aware, 2) Recognizing and Defining Terms, and 3) Finding Processes of Seeking and Understanding Information.

STEP ONE TO COLLEGE KNOWLEDGE AND UNIVERSITY JARGON: BECOMING AWARE

The college search and application processes and the people who manage them make assumptions that all prospective students understand the nuances of higher education qualifications and requirements, financial aid systems, and institutional structures. However, the complexity of accessing college presents many roadblocks for rural students, such as Taylor and Landry at MapDot High School. Regarding higher education requirements, the rural students faced financial barriers in taking the required standardized tests; did not have the option to take AP or IB courses; and made a curricular choice of Core 4+ Academic, Core 4 Career, or Basic Core at the end of the sophomore year which determined whether or not students were qualified for college in their home state. MapDot High School students' higher education aspirations tended to be unrealistic and they, their families, and their communities did not usually have the "right kind" of cultural capital—the kind that includes college knowledge—to help frame students' expectations.

MapDot High School students were acquainted with college knowledge and university jargon at varying levels. Some students had little to no information about college and its corresponding jargon, while several students retained a common understanding of the material, and very few students possessed substantial comprehension of college knowledge and jargon. Students' levels of identification and understanding of college knowledge were often shaped by their parents and families' familiarity with higher education; students' ability to associate college information and jargon with things they already knew; the terminology universities chose for recruitment efforts; connections to people who had attended college; and students' own feelings about obtaining and comprehending college knowledge.

Access to Information and Resources

Some of the inequities in college knowledge result from rural families' inexperience or unfamiliarity with higher education processes. Parents and guardians of rural students could generally support the idea of college but could not usually provide the access to specific information or contacts that more privileged parents could offer their children, nor could rural parents give students firsthand experience with the benefits of education—they had no "when I was in college" tales to share (Chenoweth & Galliher, 2004; Dumais & Ward, 2009).

All of the students in this study, and many others at MapDot High School, would be first-generation college students per this study's definition—students who are the first in their immediate families to attend college and whose parents or guardians have no college or university experience. Students may have had grandparents, aunts, uncles, cousins, or friends of the family who attended and/or graduated from a college or university, but none of the students' parents or direct guardians had collegiate experience. This definition confused some of the students who believed one or more of their parents had college experience when, in reality, their parents had attended technical and trade schools. This study defined college or university as a two-year or four-year higher education institution that granted academic degrees. This misnomer about the definition of college hints at students' misperception of university jargon and their challenges with college knowledge.

MapDot High School students discussed if and how they spoke with their parents and guardians about college. Many of them described talking about "going to college" with their parents, but shared that they never had a real conversation about what it takes to get there—academic qualifications, applications and corresponding documents, financial aid, etc. Landry admitted that he had never really talked with his family about higher education, while Taylor explained that her mom had given her information because they did not want her to waste her time or lack focus and they strongly suggested that she start near home at a local community college. Ms. Guillory, MapDot High School's counselor, recognized that parents may not be the ideal source of information because they often did not have personal collegiate experience. She described how parents often "don't have a clue" and cannot explain things, such as the different degree options, although she noted that some parents try to learn about higher education and what it takes to be successful at a college or university. Ms. Guillory understood that not all information parents shared with students was correct, but she felt that the conversation among families was an important starting point. She also shared that parents sometimes reached out to her for help, although she estimated only 25% of parents attended school sponsored assemblies about higher education.

Although their parents did not attend college, a few of the MapDot High School students had people in their lives who had some college experience, which caused the students to view these folks as "experts" because they had at least a basic understanding of higher education. Students often mentioned these "expert" family members or friends when they discussed what, if any, information they had received about college. However, the information these "experts" provided to the rural students was mostly in the form of pep talks or support rather than actual college knowledge. Taylor described how her godmother talked to her about college and "how you have to have your head in the books and how hard it is, but that you should never give up and try your hardest." Landry discussed that his friend's brother had informed them about the number of courses required and the variety of things you can do at some colleges. Depending on one or two individuals with partial college experience for "expert" advice places limitations on rural students' college knowledge and, thus, their predisposition and search phases of college access.

Rural students' college planning behavior is shaped not only by information they have but also by the information and expectations they receive, or do not receive, from their secondary schools (McDonough, 1997). MapDot High School students responded with resounding comments of "not yet," "not really," or "nope" when asked if they had been introduced to any college information by their public high schools or counselor. A few students commented on hearing some university jargon from the counselor, during their class lessons, or when talking to public high school or district educators. However, the majority of the information they recalled receiving from their rural, public school revolved around the three academic curriculum tracks offered by MapDot High School and additional academic options such as dual enrollment with local community colleges.

Ms. Guillory was dismayed by the students' statements. She described how she has meetings with the students and their parents during eighth grade and prior to twelfth grade to discuss college or other post–high school options. She presented academic scheduling information during classes that included some college discussion and she shared about the one-on-one conversations she had with students about college; however, she did recognize that most of those conversations happen with students who are public high school seniors. There seemed to be some disconnect between what Ms. Guillory believed she was providing and what the students seemed to be taking away from their interactions with her.

Colleges and universities were not connecting with rural students either. As mentioned in chapter 2, institutions of higher education show limited interest in recruiting in rural areas, which reduces the amount of information and resources rural students receive directly from institutions. MapDot High School students, like Taylor, only received electronic and hard copy information from universities based on their extracurricular engagement. Taylor explained that she had received mailings from a couple of universities because of her attendance at cheerleading camp and some online research she had conducted about the institutions, which she believed put her on a contact list. However, most MapDot High students had not received any kind of information from colleges or universities, which may reflect institutions' shift to electronic marketing, the assumptions and expectations that students all have easy access to technology, and apathy for recruiting in rural areas.

College Knowledge and University Jargon

Chenoweth and Galliher (2004) found college knowledge to be one of "the most important problems in rural students' college decision process" (p. 13). Obtaining necessary college information is often the most difficult for the students who need it the most—including rural students. Ms. Guillory recognized MapDot High School students' lack of college knowledge and acknowledged that students have a lot to learn—including but not limited to how to plan a college schedule when so many different time and format options are available; how to make sense of credit hours; how to navigate financial aid processes; and how to generate the resilience needed to persist to graduation. She also worried that the MapDot High students depended too heavily on her and wanted them to develop more self-sufficiency around college knowledge because she would not be with them at college to walk them through it all.

Ms. Guillory's comments highlighted some of the information gaps students had about college and how students were even less familiar with specific jargon (e.g., credit hours, FAFSA, etc.). Most of the MapDot High students, when asked, could not identify any university jargon off the top of their heads, although they did throw out concepts around different degrees and sorority life. Landry commented that he heard adults say words about college but he did not know what they meant because "he's not too good with words." Ms. Guillory also frequently observed students' unfamiliarity with jargon. She specifically mentioned their challenges with terms—such as, major and minor, liberal arts, credit hours, associate's and bachelor's, degree designations (B.A. vs. B.S.), syllabus, and work study—and how sometimes the definitions "blow their minds." However, she believed the rural students understood some terms, like room, board, scholarships, semester, full-time, tuition, fees, and the state tuition opportunity program.

Ms. Guillory attributed students' challenges with university jargon to the infrequency with which they hear it and she shared that students sometimes visit her office to ask about differences between terms and academic fields of study. However, she admitted that she did not always know the terms or nuances herself and shared how sometimes she and the students were both confused.

Application processes

Overall, MapDot High School students were very unaware of the components of college application processes. Landry admitted that he did not know very much and that he could not explain anything about it. The rural students did not seem to know where to locate applications or what corresponding documents they would need to submit with the applications. Taylor seemed the most well versed in the process because she knew she could find the applications online or at the County Career Day and that she would have to submit her GPA, ACT score, resume, extracurricular activities, and basic demographic information. Taylor also discussed the concept of recommendation letters and her anxiety about asking people to write them.

However, Taylor did not know about personal statements, nor did any of her peers. Other MapDot High School students also struggled with the concepts of letters of recommendation; most students had little understanding about the letters or their purpose, which was summed up in Landry's question: "Don't your teachers or somebody else you know write them?" The students seemed skeptical about their college knowledge and most of the time they either responded to questions about the application process with their own questions or a version of "I've heard it, but I don't know what it is." This does not surprise Ms. Guillory who remarked that many of the MapDot High students came by her office to ask her how to find applications, determine if their program of interest is available at an institution, register for college, and generally inquire if she could just do the process for them.

Financial aid

MapDot High School students were more aware of financial aid than any other aspect of college knowledge, which is likely reflective of their concern about paying for college and their recognition of the financial climate in own families and the broader MapDot community. Ms. Guillory explained that students often know that financial aid means money to go to college but do not fully grasp all of its components—the state tuition opportunity program, subsidized and unsubsidized loans, grants, work study, etc.—or that the process is dependent on obtaining their parents' tax forms and completing the free application for federal student aid (FAFSA).

The MapDot High School students spoke about the financial aid process in generalities, which supported Ms. Guillory's explanations. The rural students understood that financial aid meant money for college, that it often came from governmental programs, and that it may require you to pay the money back. Taylor knew she had to apply to get financial aid and that it was money to pay for college, while Landry offered his belief that financial aid was a loan for "books and stuff" that he would have to pay back monthly when he "got himself set." This rudimentary understanding of financial aid does not allow rural students to fully benefit from all the existing aid options, misrepresents repayment plan policies, and can sometimes deter rural students from college-going, if they are particularly loan averse.

Institution/location

Rural students' knowledge of higher education institutions was entirely framed by the location of MapDot. Every rural student in the study was focused on institutions within a two-hour radius of the rural county. Though they did occasionally name the state's flagship institution, the main campus of the other state university system, and a couple of private state universities, students mostly concentrated on the two community colleges that are closest to MapDot. The two community colleges—both branch campuses in the state flagship system—are located within a 25-minute drive and a 45-minute drive, respectively, from MapDot. However, there were two exceptions to this community college mentality; Taylor did mention a passing interest in an out-of-state art and design university and another student mentioned Harvard as a joke during a counselor meeting.

University Recruitment Materials

Colleges and universities tend to assume students' level of college knowledge and familiarity with university jargon based on the terminology they use in their recruitment and admissions brochures and on their websites.

Information was requested from all of the state public and private colleges and universities to analyze the amount of university jargon incorporated into institutions' recruitment and admissions materials. Only seven of the institutions mailed the requested hard copy materials, which was an example of a barrier rural students face if they do not have access to technology.

The seven colleges and universities that did send materials were not consistent in institutional type; they were located throughout the state, were both public and private, represented both two-year and four-year colleges, and varied in size. The institutional response times varied as well. Two institutions sent electronic replies within one week, even though the request asked for hard copy materials, while the other five institutions opted for standard mail that took between one and two weeks. Five of the institutions sent only one communication (either electronic or hard copy); two of institutions continued to send information periodically. The colleges and universities that supplied information also sent it in a variety of formats. There were full-size glossy brochures, small postcards, odd-sized packets, applications, and even simple emails.

Each communication tool contained between 1 and 25 jargon terms based on the study's jargon list (see Appendix G). Even a small, four-fold brochure from one of the two community colleges most referenced by MapDot High School students and counselors used 12 jargon terms. The most prevalent terms fell into the financial jargon and degree designation jargon categories, although general university and academic jargon did appear periodically. Table 5.1 lists examples of the jargon used in the university recruitment materials.

The widespread use of jargon in university recruitment, admissions, and financial aid materials and the unfamiliarity rural students have with jargon created a convoluted experience for MapDot High School students who were trying to navigate college processes. Ms. Guillory even mentioned her frustrations with managing university websites, online documents, and the absence of hard copy materials. As such, she tried to keep printed copies of

Table 5.1 Jargon Examples from University Recruitment Materials

Type of Jargon	Example Terms Used
Financial Jargon	Financial Aid, FAFSA, Tuition, Fees, Scholarships, Grants, Loans, TOPS, Work Study, Merit-Based, Need-Based, Subsidized, Unsubsidized
Degree Jargon	Certificate, Certifications, Associate Degree, Associate of Arts, Associate of Science, Bachelor's Degree, Baccalaureate Degree, B.S., PhD
General Jargon	Faculty, College, University, Semester
Academic Jargon	ACT/SAT, AP, IB, Full-Time, Part-Time, Major, Minor, Liberal Arts, Accreditation, Credit Hours

popular academic majors and colleges in her office because she hated always having to traverse through complex university websites and believed it was much quicker and easier to find and share information in hard copy.

Emotional or Cognitive Reaction to Awareness

College knowledge and the ability to locate and learn jargon can often stir an emotional or cognitive reaction in people, as demonstrated in Ms. Guillory's frustration. People often have a reaction to their level of college knowledge; however, they are not always willing to display or reflect on those reactions. MapDot High School students resisted a discussion on their emotional or cognitive reactions to their limited college knowledge and recognition of university jargon. Many students, when asked, said they did not have any reaction to their unfamiliarity or knowledge gaps. This may be linked to their peers' influence and not realizing that many students who were their age in other parts of the state and country did possess this knowledge—a case of "you don't know what you don't know." Rural students may think and feel like it is normal not to have this knowledge because most people in their rural community do not have it and do not need to obtain it. Taylor was pragmatic about her lack of knowledge, declaring that it was normal and "just something that [she] was going to end up having to learn" because, if she intended to go to college, she would eventually have to do an application. A few students were willing to express their reactions though. "I do feel like I need to know more about going to college," Landry acknowledged, "so I can have more of a chance to get in."

Whether or not the students wanted to admit having reactions, Ms. Guillory was attuned to students' reactions and recognized that they sometimes felt nervous, insecure, overwhelmed, frustrated, and panicked. She gave the example of a student who had recently been in her office to fill out an application because the student felt they could neither understand nor complete the application on their own. Ms. Guillory advised the student to breathe and have more confidence in facing new situations. She further illustrated rural students' hesitation and panic about the "new-ness" of college by sharing how eight students engaging in dual enrollment that Fall had dropped out of the course because there were too many other students in the class and the professor had scared them; however, she also pointed out that the few who had the confidence and perseverance to stay in the course ended up loving the experience. These findings aligned with the "fear, nervousness, and surprise" that rural students in Ganss' (2016) study expressed about transitions from high school to college.

It is unclear why MapDot High students claimed to have no reaction when their counselor attested that they do, indeed, have both emotional and cognitive reactions. The issue in sharing could be attributed to many things including the students' lack of comfort in sharing personal feelings with a new person, "not knowing what they don't know," or normalizing the situation based on the community's unfamiliarity with college knowledge. Whether or not a lack of reaction was positive or negative is also open to interpretation. Some would say that rural students' not having a reaction allowed them to feel "normal" and not allow their knowledge gap to further impact their college access or the "better life" they sought. Others would suggest that students' lack of reaction exemplified how their cultural capital, habitus, and motivation could result in less motivation to learn what they needed to know to access higher education.

Whether or not students opted to share or reflect on their reaction to their understanding of college knowledge and university jargon, students' immediate reactions were apparent through their body language and other nonverbal communication. When the MapDot High School students had the opportunity to apply their ability to recognize university jargon during the initial interview, they seemed anxious about circling terms that they may later have to define and inquired about the parameters of "knowing a word." Then, during the second interview's defining jargon exercise, there were many anxious and frustrated exhalations. Students seemed nervous about stating definitions incorrectly and remorseful about not being able to define more terms. So, despite their claims to not have a reaction to their knowledge level, the students' nonverbal communication relayed a reaction that often matched how their counselor described their responses to dealing with college knowledge and university jargon in an everyday setting.

STEP TWO TO COLLEGE KNOWLEDGE AND UNIVERSITY JARGON: RECOGNIZING AND DEFINING TERMS

MapDot High School students were given the opportunity to demonstrate if and how they recognized and defined university jargon from prepared lists (see Appendix G) on two different occasions. The lists contained university jargon in four different areas of college knowledge—1) general jargon, 2) academic jargon, 3) financial jargon, and 4) degree designation jargon. The first exercise asked students to circle any term that they recognized and thought they could define; the second exercise asked them to write the definition next to each word that they thought they could define.

Recognition of Terms

During the jargon recognition exercise, students were asked to *circle any term with which they were familiar* and thought they could explain. There were 54 total jargon terms on the list. Table 5.2 represents how many terms were included in each jargon category.

All participants in the study circled five of the jargon terms—faculty, staff, semester, scholarships, and the state tuition assistance program—which indicated that the students felt they could define those terms. No participant circled the following 15 terms—PWI, HBCU, HSI, AANAPI, IB, degree audit, prerequisite, syllabus, FAFSA, TRiO, A.A., A.S., A.A.S., B.A., or B.S.—which indicated that students were completely unfamiliar with these terms.

Table 5.3 represents each participant's awareness of the terms within each jargon category; the numbers designate how many terms the students circled in each category. Overall, the students most readily recognized terms in the financial jargon category. It was not surprising that students were most familiar with this category; their social class and the financial climate in their families and the broader, rural community heighten their financial concerns about college. It also made sense that students were least familiar with degree jargon because these terms were rarely, if ever, discussed on the high school level, as noted by Ms. Guillory earlier in this chapter.

Definition of Terms

During the jargon definition experience, students were asked to *write the definition* for any term with which they were familiar and thought they could describe. There were, again, 54 total jargon terms on the list, with a certain number of terms in each category (see Table 5.2).

Table 5.2   The Number of Jargon Terms by Category

Category	General Jargon	Academic Jargon	Financial Jargon	Degree Jargon	Total Jargon
Number of Terms	14	22	10	8	54

Table 5.3   Students' Total Jargon Term Recognition during Interview #1

Student	General Jargon	Academic Jargon	Financial Jargon	Degree Jargon	Total Jargon
Participant #1	9	15	7	3	34/54 = 63%
Participant #2	5	14	7	2	28/54 = 52%
Participant #3	5	14	6	0	25/54 = 46%
Participant #4	7	9	5	2	23/54 = 43%
Participant #5	6	4	5	1	16/54 = 30%
Participant #6	6	7	5	1	19/54 = 35%
Participant #7	8	8	6	3	25/54 = 46%
Participant #8	6	11	5	3	25/54 = 46%
Totals	52/112 = 46%	82/176 = 47%	46/80 = 58%	15/64 = 23%	

This time there were only two terms—ACT and semester—that all eight participants could define. No participant attempted to define the following 25 terms—Public, PWI, HBCU, HSI, AANAPI, IB, accredited, liberal arts, general education, degree audit, prerequisite, section, drop/add, syllabus, FAFSA, work study, TRiO, A.A., A.S., A.A.S., B.A., B.S., master's, doctoral, and professional.

Table 5.4 represents each student's definitions of the jargon within each category; the numbers designate how many terms the students defined completely or partially correct in each category. Similar to the recognition activity, the rural students were most familiar with terms in the financial jargon category.

Again, it was not surprising that students were most proficient with financial jargon because financial concerns topped their list of college access challenges. Students' definitions were counted as completely correct, accurate enough to be considered correct, or incorrect. For example, correct definitions for scholarship could be listed by students as "money for college," "a reward that is given to pay for school," "money given to a student to pay for their education," or "where a college or university pays for half of your college funds."

The majority of the jargon MapDot High School students chose to define were terms about which they felt relatively confident. They tended to leave jargon terms blank if they did not know them rather than guessing the definition, although a couple of students did take that approach once or twice. It was clear that students preferred leaving jargon definitions blank over submitting speculations or incorrect answers.

Table 5.4   Students' Total Jargon Term Recognition during Interview #2

Student	General	Academic	Financial	Degree	Total
Participant #1	4	3	2	0	9/54 = 17%
Participant #2	2	3	3	0	8/54 = 15%
Participant #3	4	13	4	0	21/54 = 39%
Participant #4	4	4	3	0	11/54 = 20%
Participant #5	7	3	2	0	12/54 = 22%
Participant #6	4	5	4	0	13/54 = 24%
Participant #7	4	7	3	0	14/54 = 26%
Participant #8	0	5	4	0	9/54 = 17%
Totals	29/112 = 26%	43/176 = 24%	25/80 = 31%	0/64 = 0%	

Counselor Insights

Ms. Guillory thought it made sense that students were most capable of both recognizing and defining financial jargon and least capable of both recognizing and defining degree designation jargon:

[It is] because they worry about financial aid. [It is] from society and their parents. They all know that it'll take money to go to college and their parents know that too. So, it's an awareness they already have and they'll start asking me, "When can I apply for financial aid?" at the beginning of their senior year. Well, baby, you need to wait until after your parents do their taxes. So, we're looking at February.

Ms. Guillory also described why she believed the rural students were least adept with terms regarding degree designations; she cited lack of parental knowledge, students' inattention to information she provided, not having available "checklists for different degrees," and the topic not being part of everyday conversations. She explained: "people don't just say, 'I'm a nurse. I have an associate degree. I'm a nurse, but I have a bachelor's degree.' It's not part of everyday conversation. You know what I'm saying?"

Overall, Ms. Guillory was mindful that the MapDot High School students do not likely compare well to their peers in understanding college knowledge and university jargon. She estimated that the rural students' knowledge of college and jargon was "average in terms of the county; below average state-wide; and below average nationally." The main reason she attributed to students' struggle with jargon was the rurality of the area: "[It's] because it's so rural. If you live in a college town you're gonna hear and see more [about college] and there's usually more educated parents in a college town," she reasoned.

Awareness vs. Comprehension

Having the MapDot High School students in this study complete exercises of recognizing and defining jargon provided insight into their levels of awareness about and comprehension of jargon. It was apparent that having to actually provide a definition for the jargon was more daunting for students. The difference between the recognition and definition exercises indicated that MapDot High students overestimated their knowledge of jargon, because their overall knowledge of jargon decreased by almost half between the jargon recognition exercise and the jargon definition exercise. As with much knowledge elicitation, it is easier to just recall seeing something—like jargon—than it is to properly define it.

Another possibility was that students may be able to identify the term but have difficulty translating their understanding into words. Landry was an example of this, offering: "I know what they [the terms] are, I just can't get the definition out." Taylor's comments also showed that she was resolved to summon all college knowledge she possessed; while completing the jargon definition exercise, she commented: "I know some of these but, I don't know [how to explain] . . . I don't want to give up . . . I will be racking my brain all day, all week."

STEP THREE TO COLLEGE KNOWLEDGE AND UNIVERSITY JARGON: FINDING PROCESSES OF SEEKING AND UNDERSTANDING INFORMATION

What was evident from steps one and two—becoming aware of jargon and recognizing and defining jargon—was that additional college knowledge needed to be acquired. Taylor, Landry, and Ms. Guillory offered several processes that MapDot High School students used to seek further information and increase their understanding of college knowledge and university jargon.

Processes

Although they "don't know what they don't know," MapDot High School students and their counselor discussed using association and common sense; asking counselors, other public high school personnel, family members, "experts," and peers; using the media and internet; and going directly to the source—colleges and universities—as processes to seek and understanding college information.

Association and Common Sense

A couple of the study participants believed that college knowledge and university jargon were concepts they could grasp through common sense or by associating the concepts with others they already knew. Landry was a strong proponent of this process. "Off the top of my head most of the [jargon terms] aren't really that hard," he asserted, adding:

> Most of the [jargon] is common sense. I can't explain [it] but I know [what it is]. Yeah, all the letters [acronyms] can be confusing: A.A., A.S., A.A.S ... I know what B.S. means, just not by these [jargon] terms! [*laughing*] I know a semester is longer than a quarter. I know full-time from part-time because of my job. I mean, if you go by common sense—what it [financial aid] has in the name—I mean if you're getting aid financially, you're getting a little bit of money just to help out.

Taylor also believed in the use of common association. She offered that the jargon could sometimes be common sense and that she had previously heard some of the terms.

Inquiring/Asking

The majority of MapDot High School students believed that the most use-ful method of increasing college knowledge and decoding university jargon would be asking someone—or checking the internet—about it. Ms. Guillory explained that students' inquiries depended on what they were doing and who else was present; she also noted that some students would ask their peers, maybe their teachers, her [the counselor], or a parent, but others would not ask at all. Landry shared that he was not sure to whom or where to go for the best source of college information but that he would probably begin the process with a person: "anyone in generally, probably." Other participants had concrete ideas about who they would ask or to what resource they would turn, including but not limited to their counselors, other public high school personnel, family members, "experts" (as mentioned earlier in this chapter and below), and peer groups.

The rural students affirmed that their public high school counselor was the primary, useful resource for them; they specifically named Ms. Guillory as a chief information source about college knowledge and university jargon. In addition to one-on-one conversations, the counselor also provided a "career center" in her office for students to browse at their own leisure, where they could review pamphlets, websites, available scholarships, and general financial aid information.

Students mentioned other MapDot High School personnel as potential, general sources of college information as well. They talked about having individual conversations with teachers and other personnel, and they recalled having a few class discussions about college knowledge and university jargon. Ms. Guillory illustrated: "[Students] will ask some [questions] of their teachers . . . teachers here are close to the kids and some are very resource-ful." MapDot High students distinctively named their principal multiple times as a willing and able resource. It seemed that the rural students had access to and were comfortable in approaching their principal. The new state man-date that all public high school students take the ACT as part of graduation requirements (see chapter 7) also helps facilitate some college conversations around the school.

The MapDot county school district also hosted a Career Day each year for all of the junior and senior students in the county. The district invited all types of postsecondary providers to attend, including but not limited to two-year colleges, four-year colleges and universities, various military branches, technical and trade schools, and public service organizations (police, fire, etc.). Students had the opportunity to explore various occupational pathways. Ms. Guillory described County Career Day as students' opportunity to meet with all the various recruiters through three 10-minute conversation sessions at recruiter booths/tables and a general browsing period. She recounted that many eleventh graders get overwhelmed because it is their first time at the career day, but attending twice allows them to hone in on their conversations choices when they attend as twelfth graders.

In addition to educators, many students named family members as people who they would turn to with college knowledge and university jargon questions or concerns, even though parents and other family members may have never been to college. Several students identified their mother as their first point of contact about college knowledge and a few also mentioned siblings, whether or not those individuals had any collegiate experience.

A few students also talked about people—both family members and acquaintances—who they knew had experience with college; they mentioned these people as resources from whom they could learn college knowledge and university jargon. MapDot High School students seemed to view these people as experts, as mentioned earlier; however, "expert" very loosely described the level of proficiency of these individuals because many of them attended technical or trade schools rather than two- or four-year colleges and a number of them did not actually graduate from any postsecondary institution. Landry described how he could probably ask his brother about jargon because his brother was "in a college for a bit and should know what some of that stuff means" even though the brother did not complete any certificate or degree program. Landry also named his friend's brother as a resource expert; however, that individual was only in his first semester of college. There were a few appropriate resources on the students' "expert" lists though. Taylor discussed using her godmother as an expert because she attended and graduated from a state HBCU in the past decade.

Though not a very widespread tactic, a couple of students did name their peers at MapDot High School as assets in acquiring and comprehending college knowledge and decoding university jargon. Taylor mentioned that some of her friends talked about it and Landry described how he could turn to some of the seniors at MapDot High for information. Ms. Guillory also brought up the concept of peer-to-peer education about college; however, she seemed to think the concept was used more frequently than it was in reality because students rarely discussed having these types of conversations with their peers.

Most, if not all, of the rural students mentioned turning to the internet and other forms of media for information and college "research." Google, as society's primary search engine, was an obvious resource for students. Landry emphasized that Google has "everything, any answer you need." MapDot High students also said they would use online dictionaries and university websites. Taylor offered that she had seen and learned jargon from online books and web searches. Additionally, a couple of students shared that they see commercials on television about admissions, financial aid, and other college knowledge and jargon. Landry claimed to learn some jargon from TV

shows and movies that featured college students and faculty. While he did
not mention which particular shows or movies he used as educational tools,
it is concerning that he may be using media that is misrepresenting higher
education.

As mentioned earlier in this chapter, some colleges and universities are
also sending information to rural students in both electronic and hard copy
formats based on their participation in extracurricular activities and, more
rarely, their academic achievements. Taylor mentioned that a state public university about an hour from MapDot sent her mailings to "check out a career
day thing" and informed her of the programs they offered. She also discussed
the institution's admissions officers and the use of jargon in both documents
and conversations:

> I see a lot of these [jargon] words on applications, college brochures, informa-
> tion . . . I read a few applications and I've asked questions [to the admissions
> professionals] and they told me [what the jargon meant]. Sometimes they tell
> you what you need [to know]. People tell [me] because I ask a lot of questions.

Ms. Guillory also described how colleges and universities, as well as
professional organizations, were resources for college knowledge and
university jargon. She noted the [State] Association of College Registrars
and Admissions Offices as a source of information. The association hosts a
workshop for all state high school counselors every year where counselors
can meet with state college and university recruiters and ACT representatives to learn about institutional admissions requirements, degree offerings,
student affairs, etc. Ms. Guillory also mentioned that local college recruiters
would be willing to visit the school on request. However, it was unclear
how often this actually occurred because, during the period of the study, the
only recruiter seen at MapDot High School was a U.S. Army recruiter. In
addition to students and their counselors using a variety of processes to gain
awareness and comprehension of college knowledge and university jargon,
an assortment of teaching and learning formats were used to acquire higher
education information.

Teaching and Learning Formats

Ms. Guillory most often imparted information through one-on-one conversations or presentations with students and, less frequently, parents. Some
students also sought out Ms. Guillory on their own to gain more knowledge.
Regardless of whether information was provided proactively or reactively,
there was a debate about whether information was most accessible and best
articulated in online or hard copy formats.

Presentations and Assemblies/Meetings

College knowledge and university jargon were typically presented to students, and sometimes their parents/families, in two primary formats—1) classroom presentations and 2) meetings or assemblies that often included both students and parents. Ms. Guillory hosted two nights of standard meetings about postsecondary options. The first meeting was held during students' eighth grade year when the counselor introduced the three academic tracks the state allows for public high school students—Core 4 Academic, Core 4 Career, and Basic Core—and the corresponding graduation requirements. The second meeting was held during students' twelfth grade year and covered postsecondary opportunities and financial aid options, including the state tuition assistance program. Student and parent involvement and engagement in the meetings varied. Some years, MapDot High School parents showed high interest in these meetings and other years only a small percentage of parents actually attended.

There were also other opportune times when Ms. Guillory presented college knowledge and university jargon to MapDot High students. "When I gave out the PLAN test, which is the 10th grade pre-ACT, I talked to them then about postsecondary [options] and the interest inventory and how we were going to use it," she noted. Ms. Guillory also capitalized on an opportunity for college counseling when she helped to recruit students for this study. While she was handing out consent forms in a classroom, the teacher turned the conversation to college planning and Ms. Guillory was open to a spontaneous counseling session. She explained that students' sophomore year was the prime time to evaluate their postsecondary options, and she brought up the topic of the state's tuition assistance program and gave the students space to ask questions, although none were raised. It seemed that students in the class were either unprepared or unwilling to ask questions at that time.

1-on-1 Meetings

At MapDot High School, Ms. Guillory arranged one-on-one meetings with all the eleventh and twelfth graders at the school. She described how the meetings were discussions of grades, curriculum checklists, diploma choices, and potentially a state tuition opportunity program checklist. Parents were only included if students wanted to opt out of the Core 4 academic tracks. Ms. Guillory noted that these meetings took a long time and, thus, she is not able to conduct similar ones with students earlier in their high school careers.

Some rural students, and even parents, took it upon themselves to seek out Ms. Guillory for further postsecondary direction and advice on college knowledge and university jargon. She explained that much of that kind of interaction is impromptu, although some students are "frequent fliers" who she "can't get rid of" and saw once or twice a week. Others students never sought her out outside of their required meetings. Ms. Guillory saw students' initiative, or lack thereof, as a sign of their level of seriousness about higher education, and she believed students paid the most attention to what she shared when they were the ones initiating contact. She maintained that it was not her job to "hunt students down" because they "knew where her office was" and she had plenty of other duties to fulfill (see chapter 6).

Assessment of Resources

Ms. Guillory was a bit dismayed about students' impression of resources. She was unsure if students were even aware of all the available resources and she had no idea if students would deem the available resources sufficient. She also had some concerns with her own resources, particularly the format in which she received information from institutions of higher education. Ms. Guillory seemed to be adapting more slowly to the change in college knowledge formats than students, who tended to seek out online resources. She shared that the move to online ACT form submissions complicated the process for MapDot High students and had increased student traffic in her office for use of its two student computers—and sometimes her own as a third. She also disliked that institutions no longer provided hard copy academic catalogs because she found it much easier to find and present information to students in hard copy.

However, rural students at MapDot High School felt relatively positive about the amount of resources they had available to them and they seemed to believe they had adequate access to those resources. Landry noted that he felt like there were a lot of available resources and he could get information if he needed, wanted, and asked for it. Taylor was the outlier of participants; she did not believe there were enough resources and she suggested that MapDot High add "more classes that would teach [college knowledge]." Process and formats for the teaching and learning of college knowledge and university jargon could be expanded or reshaped to better serve both rural students and their counselors.

CONCLUSION

College knowledge and university jargon present challenges for rural students as they navigate their college predisposition and search phases and rely on cultural capital that does not align well with higher education's middle- and upper-class mindset. However, rural students can and do seek out ways to grow their college knowledge and ability to decode university jargon by becoming more aware, increasing their ability to recognize and define terms, and finding new processes of seeking and understanding information. One of their key resources—their public high school counselor—faced challenges of her own, though, which impacted her ability to fully serve the students' college-going needs. The public high school counselor's role is addressed in chapter 6.

Chapter 6

"I Have More to Do Than I Can Possibly Do Well"

Rural Counselors' Challenges with College Counseling

Many of the challenges that rural students face with college access and college knowledge could potentially be addressed in the public high school environment by counselors. Specifically, counselors could be educating rural students on the academic, financial, and social aspects of their college search and choice (Hossler & Gallagher, 1987) and providing suggestions on how to make informed, rational decisions that could result in higher rates of college entrance and persistence (Bickel at al., 1991; Paulsen & Loflink, 2005). However, McDonough et al. (2010) point out that counselors tend to have limited college knowledge and only provide information about higher education institutions in the specific rural area or its adjacent areas. MapDot High School and its counselor faced similar constraints because Ms. Guillory had to simultaneously provide numerous services to students—including college counseling—while also trying to keep herself current on college knowledge and university jargon.

COUNSELOR MENTALITY

Ms. Guillory is a native of the rural area. She attended high school at the county's one private school, and after obtaining a bachelor's degree in elementary education in the 1980s, she immediately returned to the rural county to work in the public school system. Ms. Guillory admits that she "went into education because it was one of the easier majors to get into and it was a good fit anyway since I didn't care for foreign language and statistics." MapDot High School having a "homegrown" counselor supports research findings that show teachers, counselors, and administrators in rural schools are often originally from the communities in which they work (Theobald & Siskar, 2008; Schafft & Jackson, 2010).

As a teacher, the now counselor saw that the rural students needed someone to talk to and someone to advocate for them, yet they had no one. That was Ms. Guillory's driver to pursue a master's degree in guidance and counseling at a public state university within an hour of the county. Once she had the master's degree in hand, she assumed the role as the sole counselor in the same school where she had been teaching since the early 1990s—MapDot High School—the place where she continues to serve to this day.

COUNSELOR ROLE(S)

Like many educators in rural areas, the rural, high school counselor is expected to perform multiple roles for the high school (Rosales, 2015). Ms. Guillory shared how she "has a lot of hats" including roles guiding and scheduling the academic curriculum, coordinating standardized tests, handling attendance issues, providing personal and career counseling to students, and contributing to many of the "paperwork processes" for students and the school's main office. These numerous roles could each be very time consuming and required lots of effort and collaboration. Much of the time Ms. Guillory felt overwhelmed by her multiple roles and the corresponding expectations. She explained:

> It's too many expectations, especially with the number of high school students that we have. Before [2004] we didn't have the computer work and paperwork that we have today. Now it's just more and more and more. You used to have one diploma track and last year we had four and now we're back to three again. It's keeping track of all that. You didn't have all these pathways that [students] have to meet. You didn't have required ACT testing. I had to give the ASVAB [military] test this morning. I only had two testers and we needed three. It's just constant.

Ms. Guillory experienced a lot of pressure to perform well in all of her roles and she believed she had "more to do than it was possible to do well." She acknowledged that the personal and career counseling for students was probably the most important component of her job, but she also admitted that it is also the aspect of her job that is often neglected because of time constraints. While Ms. Guillory's tasks and, thus, time commitments fluctuated daily and also with the ebb and flow of the school calendar, she did note that paperwork took up more time than she liked—and way more time than most of her colleagues realized.

College Counseling

One of the many services that Ms. Guillory provided to MapDot High School was college counseling. The extent of college counseling that she offered to MapDot High students varied by time of year, the number of school changes and crises to which she had to attend, and students' interest. Ms. Guillory estimated that she spent between 5% and 40% of her time on discussing higher education with the rural students, depending on the time of year and the time she had to give. She explained that the eleventh and twelfth graders at MapDot High are typically the ones with questions and she opened her office to the students—even giving up her own computer at times—so they could have internet access to engage in the college search and application processes. Ms. Guillory characterized her office as a comforting place for students as they try to manage the panic of accessing college, and she described herself as a resource to guide them through the complex online application processes, even though she really believed that students have the capacity to navigate it on their own. Because she tried to give such personalized attention to students who seek her out for college counseling, Ms. Guillory knew that she should spend more of her time on these efforts for all students if time permitted, but it usually did not.

Tasks that comprised Ms. Guillory's college counseling efforts included but were not limited to: holding meetings with students and parents (particularly eighth and twelfth graders); providing resources such as websites; assisting students with standardized testing, college applications, scholarship applications, and financial aid forms; explaining university jargon; interpreting careers and occupational duties; scheduling campus visits; and connecting students with career role models. Ms. Guillory illustrated her personal touch through stories about how parents would send her their tax forms in order for her to complete the FAFSA process on the family's behalf and how she would work with admissions staff at the local community colleges to get personalized tours scheduled for MapDot High School students. It was clear that she wanted to help the rural students and families who sought her out; however, one could argue that the ones not asking for the assistance on their own might need it even more.

OVERLOAD: RATIOS AND SHORT-STAFFING

Public schools often have an average student-to-counselor ratio of 500:1, even though the American School Counselor Association (ASCA) recommends only a 250:1 ratio (Harris, 2014; Rosales, 2015; National Center for Educational Statistics, 2006). These numbers represent the difficulty students have in seeking time-intensive help from their school counselors. The situation at MapDot High School mirrored the national landscape with a student-to-counselor ratio of 450:1. Ms. Guillory agreed with the ASCA recommendations and believed that the ratio at MapDot High was daunting in light of all of the responsibilities that rural, public high school counselors were expected to handle.

In MapDot, Ms. Guillory could also be called on to serve students outside of the public high school at times. While her actual job was to serve as the full-time high school counselor, she explained that MapDot Middle School only had a part-time counselor, so on Tuesdays and Thursdays Ms. Guillory was also the counselor for an additional 400 middle school students. This larger 850:1 ratio was higher than national average and thwarted the ASCA recommendations, highlighting that many rural schools are short-staffed in the counselor role. In addition, unlike some suburban and urban schools that employ counseling support staff, Ms. Guillory had no administrative or other type of staff who worked in her area; she was the only individual managing all of the counseling tasks for MapDot High School (and sometimes middle school). For this reason and many others, scholars call for the hiring of additional counselors and support staff who can make a special effort to provide underrepresented students with the counseling and college knowledge they need to turn their educational aspirations into realities (Bickel et al., 1991; Paulsen & Loflink, 2005).

Community colleges are beginning to realize the staffing issue in their local public high school counseling offices and are creating positions called College Coaches—individuals whom the community colleges assign to go into specific counties or high schools for one or two days a week to help students with college preparation and ease the burden of the one public high school counselor. MapDot High School received assistance from one of these College Coaches during this study; however, the individual was not available to provide further explanation of the new program or her experiences with the MapDot High School students. Ms. Guillory did not comment on whether or not she believed the College Coach at MapDot High School was impacting her workload or the students' understanding of college processes.

COUNSELOR RESOURCE IMBALANCES

Unlike their rural counterparts, students at affluent, private, and "college preparatory" high schools often have counselor ratios that align with the ASCA recommendation, counselors devoted solely to college counseling, and counseling staffs that include paraprofessionals and support staff to manage paperwork and serve as front-line employees. Lower ratios, more staff, and individuals dedicated to the singular role of college counselor allow other high school counselors to provide proactive and more complete college counseling programs. McDonough (1997) showcased the imbalances between well-resourced and under-resourced high schools, where well-resourced counselors talked about offering career testing, creating new college handbooks and guides each year for the junior class, organizing school-only college fairs, hosting financial aid and personal statement writing workshops, writing individualized recommendation letters, and spending at least 10–15 hours providing college-counseling services to each student.

Counselors in well-resourced schools with higher rates of college-going tend to also have ample opportunities for professional development to stay current on higher education trends and changes, including courting by colleges and universities who fly counselors in for training and to market their institutions (McDonough, 1997; personal communication, December 30, 2015). In many cases, counselors and high schools with ample resources have more access to further resources while those who struggle—rural, public schools like MapDot High—do not get invited to participate.

CONCLUSION

Public high school guidance counselors—such as Ms. Guillory—are often one of the few informed higher education resources to which rural students have access. Counselors have a significant influence not only on individual students but also on the college-going culture of the public high school and even the broader community (McDonough, 1997). Therefore, when counselors face limitations in human, information, and time resources because of their multiple roles and expectations, students are left to figure out the college search and choice processes on their own—or abandon the idea altogether. This is why depending on only the public high school counselor to aid students in their college access, search, and choice processes is misguided. Rather, all educators, community members, and policymakers should strive to bolster rural students' college aspirations and access, which is the focus of chapter 7.

Aspirations and Access Assignments for Everyone in Education

Strategies for Rural, Public High Schools, Rural Communities, Higher Education, and Policymakers

College access and choice is not only a higher education issue but also a PK-16 pipeline concern and a public policy matter. Many families and policymakers in the United States consider higher education an essential component of personal and community success and want more access and choice options (Hossler & Palmer, 2012). Additionally, because high schools are being evaluated for quality based on the number of students they guide to colleges and universities, it is imperative to focus on college knowledge and access, regardless of geographic region or resource availability (Hossler & Palmer, 2012). Educating citizens should be a critical issue for all people and a permanent topic of interest in U.S. politics and government because of the positive outcomes associated with higher education—for both the private good and the public good.

POLICY IMPLICATIONS

From the historical Morrill Acts of 1862 and 1890, *Brown v. Board of Education* (1954) decision, and Civil Rights Act of 1964 to the more recent No Child Left Behind Act (2001) and divestment of higher education at both the federal and state levels, governmental policy has long played a central role in and had significant impact on how the PK-12 and higher education systems operate. During this study, the state made two policy decisions—requirement of ACT testing for all students and proposed elimination of the high school counselor position—that had considerable influence on how public, rural high schools were assessed, how they prepared students for higher education, and what role, if any, public high school counselors would retain.

ACT Requirement in State's Public High Schools

During spring 2012 the State Department of Education (State DOE) decided to replace the former state standardized test with the ACT (Gentzel, 2012). The new rule was implemented in spring 2013 and required all students in public schools in the state to take the series of ACT tests including the EXPLORE and PLAN pre-exams during eighth, ninth, and tenth grades leading up to the actual ACT test during the eleventh grade (Genztel, 2012; Sentell, 2012). The ACT costs were subsidized by the state; all students could take the test once at no cost and students who qualified for federal free or reduced lunch were eligible for two additional attempts at the standardized exam (Sentell, 2012). Administration of the test occurred during school hours. This decision was an effort by the state to "change the cycle" because "the state still has *the smallest percentage of households in the country* where at least one adult has an associate or bachelor's degree . . . and 17 percent of children live in a home headed by a high school dropout" (Sentell, 2012, emphasis in original). Some district superintendents believed this change was a good decision because it forced students to take the ACT and it could potentially help more rural students envision themselves as college material (Advocate Editorial, 2016; Genztel, 2012).

Based on this study's findings, the State DOE requirement of ACT testing would, at least, make rural students aware of the ACT test and give them access to take it, up to three times at no cost, which would complete a college admission requirement. The change could have also fostered earlier conversations about higher education, college knowledge, and university jargon because the EXPLORE exam is first administered during eighth grade. These two advantages may help rural students obtain and comprehend more college knowledge and university jargon and may encourage—or force—counselors to spend a bit more time on the college counseling portion of their role.

However, there were also several potential unintended consequences of this new State DOE rule. If rural students' ACT scores were low they may be even less inclined to pursue higher education than they were before, feeling like they are not academically capable based on a test that is known to be regionally, racially, and culturally biased. Even before the State DOE rule change went into effect, Ms. Guillory, the MapDot High School counselor, pointed out that the students at MapDot High tended to have low ACT scores, with some students only scoring a 12 out of the possible 36. Receiving low scores on pre-ACT exams as early as eighth grade may demotivate students from academic pursuits and dissuade them from even considering higher education. Making it mandatory for all public high school students to take the ACT could also drive the state's already low ranking (44th nationally) in ACT scoring to drop even further because all students would be taking the exam instead of only those who are self-selecting it (Sentell, 2012). Additionally, the State DOE altered its school performance scoring system to include students' scores on the ACT as 25% of the overall school performance score (Sentell, 2012). The hope was that the incorporation of the ACT on the school performance score would entice schools to make the ACT exam a priority and focus within the state's public high schools.

The ACT requirement put further pressure on rural schools because it added responsibilities to the counselor's role, did not take into account the disparity in academic offerings—AP, IB, dual enrollment, etc.—between school districts, and did not account for the number of students who are enrolled in the Basic Core academic track. Ms. Guillory was highly concerned about the school performance score at MapDot High School declining because of the high number of students at MapDot High who were not even on track to get a high school diploma yet were required to take the ACT. There was also a question about which employee(s) at the public high schools would administer the ACT testing system because, though counselors had previously served as standardized test coordinators and administrators, there was a State Board of Elementary and Secondary Education (State BOE) proposal to change the State School Handbook for School Administrators rule about the presence and functions of public high school counselors.

Overall, the new State DOE rule resulted in some marginal improvements. In 2016, "25,144 students in the state earned an ACT score of 18 or higher," which was an improvement of "462 students from 2015, 959 students from 2014, and of 6,312 students from 2012," before the ACT requirement went into effect (McGill, 2015, para. 8; Sentell, 2016, para. 8–9). When compared with other states who require the ACT test in high school, this state ranks 13th out of the 17 and students' average composite scores (19.5) rank in the 30th percentile nationally, which the State Superintendent of Education considers real progress (Advocate Editorial, 2016). Overall, the number of students who earned college-qualifying scores has risen 37 percent since the ACT testing requirement went into effect (Sentell, 2016).

Despite the supposed increase in college-readiness, as determined by standardized testing, the State Superintendent did acknowledge that withdrawal rates from state higher education institutions were still dismal. Thus, the assessment of whether the ACT requirement is truly beneficial for rural students and actually measures college-readiness cannot yet be determined, and college enrollment and withdrawal data by county and high school are needed to assess if there have been increases in college aspiration and attendance for students from rural areas.

State BOE Proposed Policy to Eliminate Public High School Counselors

In fall 2012, the State BOE discussed changes to the State School Handbook for School Administrators. The crucial change being deliberated was whether or not to continue requiring PK-12 schools in the state to employ counselors. There was heated discussion across the state, including on the local news and in local papers around MapDot, about the proposed change, particularly from counselors and even within the State BOE. Despite the concerns, the State BOE approved the proposition in January 2013 with the added caveat that schools were not allowed to completely eliminate the counselor position but, rather, could outsource the roles of a counselor to third parties in lieu of hiring a full-time counselor for the school (Sentell, 2013). Effectively, the changes to the handbook diminished the role of counselors in state public high schools (Sentell, 2013). The State Superintendent of Education called the change "a bid to trim the role of the state on a wide array of mandates and give local educators more authority" (Sentell, 2013, para. 8). However, there was no direction from the state on quality vendors that schools could, or should, utilize to outsource counseling services nor was there any accountability that the third parties would necessitate the same training and credentials typically required of traditional high school counselors.

Counselors were infuriated by the State BOE approval of the change. A quote from one counselor stated: "I beg you, I plead with you, please don't take a step backwards," while another appealed: "Please don't fail [the state] students now" (Sentell, 2013, para. 14–16). The counselors recognized the essential role they played in public high schools and the variety of services that would cease to exist, or move to other administrators' jobs, should schools opt for outsourcing. MapDot High School's counselor, Ms. Guillory, shared many examples of the crucial roles that counselors fill, particularly in rural, public high schools. Trying to outsource or find other personnel to handle all these various functions—standardized test coordination, attendance, academic scheduling, personal counseling, college counseling, career counseling, administration of paperwork, etc.—would be a major transition for public high schools and likely could end up costing the high school or district more than the counselors' salaries.

The State BOE policy completely contrasted the findings of this study. Rural students were heavily reliant on their public high school counselors for a variety of services—including college counseling. They were comfortable with their counselors because they built a personal relationship with them and because the counselors were natives to the rural area. Their comfort facilitated their inquiry to counselors about higher education options and information. Both counselors and students were clear that the counselor played a central role in students', and even parents', acquisition and command of college knowledge. This was demonstrated through Ms. Guillory helping families with FAFSA forms and walking students through application processes, among other forms of college access assistance. The State BOE's change may have directly impact if, or how, students received college counseling. The effect of the alteration in the handbook is still not fully known. However, both this policy and the ACT test policy were governmental decisions with practical implications for how both rural counselors and students handled higher education preparation. In the future, it may behoove state policymakers to learn about the lived experiences of students and counselors and inquire about potential drawbacks of proposed policy changes before making such impactful decisions.

PRACTICAL IMPLICATIONS

Schools are an example of the institutionalized effects of cultural capital, which shapes students' educational aspirations (Tramonte & Willms, 2009). The findings of this study inform school districts, rural public high schools, high school counselors, and colleges and universities about the college information needs of rural students and which processes and resources may best assist with information acquisition. Data from this study provided insight into rural students' need to have choices in processes and resources that focus on both micro and macro levels including the individual, family, school, and entire community. Data also revealed key relationships that were central to students' processes of decoding university jargon, including students' level of comfort with counselors and access to higher education "experts" or role models. Parents, families, school personnel, and community members need to be included in the conversations and educational programs that rural students receive about university jargon and college knowledge to help build both the family and community's cultural capital and support students' college aspirations and access.

The exploration of processes students used to decode university jargon (see chapter 5) raises awareness that jargon is sometimes a true impediment to rural students' college knowledge. Students discussed their confusion around jargon and were uneasy about being asked to define terms, and their counselor affirmed that they had a lot to learn about college knowledge and university jargon. Additionally, the study uncovered gaps in students' processes of decoding university jargon, including counselors' limited time and resources; students' need to further develop the "right kind" of cultural capital and college knowledge; students' feeling that not knowing jargon was "normal"; institutions' use of university jargon without explanation in recruitment materials; and disinterest from college and university recruiters in visiting rural areas. Students' behavior was shaped not only by information they had but also by the information and expectations they did not receive (McDonough, 1997). Overall, this study helps to inform secondary and higher education scholars and practitioners about processes of building additional cultural capital, which allows both rural counselors and students to decode university jargon and increase their comprehension of college knowledge.

Assistance for Counselors

This study revealed the challenges rural, public high school counselors have with managing all the various roles that they are expected to fill (see chapter 6). College counseling was not always a priority for MapDot High School's counselor, Ms. Guillory, for a multitude of legitimate reasons, including but not limited to a shortage of staff, too many roles, and a lack of all kinds of resources.

Staffing

Ms. Guillory mentioned how she was the sole counselor at MapDot High School. Yet, she was expected to fill many roles including academic scheduler, test administrator, administrative personnel, personal counselor, college counselor, and career counselor. Ms. Guillory admitted that she had more to do than she can possibly do well and was continuously strapped for time. It was apparent that she was stretched thin and did not always feel like she was addressing students' needs because she spent a lot of her time on administrative duties rather than meeting with students. This is particularly true of her attention to college counseling, where she noted the struggle to provide adequate information and college search resources to older students while also giving time to increase predisposition of younger students. Findings from this study suggest that public high schools should increase counselor staffing, seek volunteer assistance from local college graduates, and/or request additional support from the new community college program to supply high schools with complementary College Coaches.

The proposition of more staffing was, and continues to be, in direct opposition to the State BOE changes to eliminate counselors or outsource the functions of counseling. However, findings from this study and other research represent the dire importance of public high school counselors and the services that they are trained to provide to students—including college counseling (Bickel et al., 1991; Hossler & Gallagher, 1987; National Center for Educational Statistics, 2006; Paulsen & Loflink, 2005). Although the study's findings do show that counselors may not have adequate time and other resources to offer comprehensive college counseling to students, what they can and do offer students is essential to students' acquisition of college knowledge and ability to decode university jargon. Data from the study speaks to students' reliance on counselors for college information and support—throughout all three stages of Hossler and Gallagher's (1987) college choice model.

Resources

Data in the study showed a shortage of higher education resources available to rural counselors. Counselors would be able to advance their college counseling practices if they had the time and financial support from their schools, district, or state to seek out additional resources. Ms. Guillory suggested several learning and growth areas for rural counselors that would benefit interactions with students including: professional development, informational handouts, college catalogs and books in hard copy, more access to technology, and the development of career centers in the rural, public high schools.

One way counselors could provide better information to rural students is if they possess better information themselves. Ms. Guillory described how she would enjoy visiting various colleges and universities to learn more about what those institutional types currently offer students; she also mentioned that conducting shadowing of different and new careers options would allow her to better explain career pathways to students and inform them of the day-to-day tasks of certain careers. Unlike counselors at elite private high schools, rural counselors do not typically have the time or resources to go on many counselor visits to colleges and universities. They also have limited knowledge about emerging career fields that may not be represented in the rural area, such as fashion and interior design or cybersecurity. It would be helpful to fund professional development opportunities and allow time away for rural counselors to broaden their knowledge base of higher education institutional types as well as emerging career fields.

Ms. Guillory shared that creating or being given informational handouts that contain and decipher college knowledge and university jargon may be helpful as well. This would allow both counselors and students to have an immediate referral resource when they came across an unfamiliar piece of information or jargon term. Counselors could also leave these types of handouts in specific areas of their offices so students could grab resources at their leisure. It would also be helpful to provide such handouts to parents, even if only during the existing eighth and twelfth grade meetings at MapDot High School.

In addition to handouts for students and parents, counselors themselves have a need for hard copies of college catalogs and career resource books. Ms. Guillory only had dated copies of such materials because most college and university catalogs and resource books are now solely in electronic formats. Students sometimes got lost or frustrated on websites when they were unsure of where to look or could not quickly find the information for which they were looking. Ms. Guillory believed that the hard copy materials were preferable because they allowed students to sit down and explore career and college options more effortlessly, particularly for schools without many computers—like MapDot High—and students who were less technologically proficient.

The use of technology was both a challenge and an opportunity for counselors. Though they wanted some things in hard copy, counselors recognized that technology could be a useful tool. For example, Ms. Guillory had two computers in her office at MapDot High School that were designated specifically for student use, although she acknowledged that two were never enough to meet the demand, which resulted in her often giving up the computer at her desk for students to be able to use it. Counselors need additional computer workstations in their offices for students to use to research higher education options, complete college applications, and apply for scholarships and financial aid. In addition to the hardware, Ms. Guillory noted that it would be beneficial to obtain career interest inventories software, have the ability to pre-load websites for students to easily access the most often visited college and scholarship websites, and allow students to watch institution's 360-degree virtual campus tours. These technological additions would fit nicely into what Ms. Guillory's idea for a MapDot High School "career center."

While Ms. Guillory had space in her office devoted to postsecondary options, it mostly consisted of hanging or stackable file folders with paperwork for scholarship applications, ACT testing materials, military recruitment information, and fliers from local trade schools. She talked about her ideas to expand this into a true career center in both space and scope. Ms. Guillory wanted to offer more information to students about possible career pathways and higher education institutions and provide ample space for them to conduct research on potential careers and corresponding schools.

Building Rural Students' Cultural Capital

This study showed students' struggles with college knowledge and university jargon, much of which related to rural students having cultural capital and habitus that are not often valued in higher education in the same way as white, middle- or upper-class norms. To enhance students' pertinent cultural capital and broaden their habitus, rural counselors suggested that students needed further interaction with role models; more engagement with "high-brow" activities; additional and repetitive exposure to college knowledge in their classrooms; and purposeful experiences that put them on college and university campuses.

Role Models

From conversations with the MapDot High School students and their counselor, it seemed that locating role models who could serve as mentors, or even just guest speakers, would support students in gathering information about college and seeing an example of someone from their rural area who completed higher education. These role models could be integrated into the students' course curriculums; for example, the school could invite doctors to come into science classes, lawyers to come into civics courses, journalists to contribute to English courses, accountants to attend math classes, and business owners to attend home economics and shop courses. Having people who have turned academic courses and interests into careers would help rural students make the connection between school and work and could also inspire students to seek further credentials—and possibly college degrees—within their academic areas of interest.

Curricular Integration

It was apparent that students received little to no information about college within their academic curriculum. The only mention of the curriculum discussing postsecondary options was the "Journey to Careers" course that students take in ninth grade; however, this course focused on students who were not in the Core 4 diploma tracks and, thus, the course mainly discussed options that did not require further education. It would be ideal if there could be a supplemental course established to discuss postsecondary options with Core 4 Academic students similar to the existing "Journey to Careers" course for Core 4 Career and Basic Core students. For example, a "Journey to Higher Education/College" course could be taught by the public high school counselor, homeroom teachers, or college-educated community volunteers to introduce college knowledge and university jargon to rural students during ninth grade and help guide them through Hossler and Gallagher's (1987) predisposition phase earlier in their high school careers. The course could contain lessons on college knowledge—academic requirements, applications, testing, personal statements, recommendation letters, financial aid, scholarships, etc.—and university jargon of all types using engaging and innovative teaching methods, such as the use of technology (including college knowledge smartphone and computer applications), mock college application processes, and class competitions about who could be first to locate the most college graduates in the community or find a mentor. The course could invite guest speakers from the rural community who have been to college or higher education representatives—like admissions recruiters—to share their college and university experiences. Campus tours to colleges and universities within an hour or two of the rural, public high school could also be incorporated. Because the Core 4 academic curriculum often leaves open spaces in students' twelfth grade academic curriculum, there should be room in the curriculum for a "Journey to Higher Education/College" course in students' ninth grade year. The addition would only require students deferring a physical education or elective course to a later year of high school.

If adding a supplemental course is not a possibility within the curriculum due to time, staffing, or lack of information/resources, it would be beneficial to build in short lessons about college knowledge and university jargon into various academic courses. There could even be an initiative once per week to open up the first five or ten minutes of each class period with a university jargon term of the week; jargon terms could be designated for each subject area and could serve as an introduction to a question and answer session about the teacher's college experience. Regardless of the pedagogical method, it is imperative that rural students receive information on college knowledge and university jargon through proactive and repetitive methods. Another way of integrating the curriculum with college knowledge and cultural capital would be to take students to "highbrow" activities or for college campus visits.

Field Trips and Campus Visits

Ms. Guillory discussed how she used to have the time and resources to bring students on field trips and/or college campus visits. She believed learning that happened off campus was valuable for students' overall experience and she wished MapDot High School could resume these kinds of activities. Ms. Guillory thought that allowing students to see other ways of being and thinking—to experience museums, historical sites, cities, and colleges and universities—pushed students to broaden their mindsets and consider new life possibilities. These kinds of activities also built students', and ultimately the community's, cultural capital and often resulted in at least a slight shift in habitus.

University Recruitment

Higher education institutions can sometimes operate on a business model that places prime value on return on investment, particularly in recruiting and admissions (see chapter 2); thus, colleges and universities often recruit student populations who have shown a tendency to enroll at their colleges and universities, which means they recruit in areas where students have a high college-going rate and where the institution is likely to see a higher yield between recruitment and enrollment. These practices result in rural students receiving infrequent—or a complete lack of—contact from most colleges and universities. Even when contact occurs, higher education recruiters and administrators do not take into account that college knowledge and university jargon may be a language that creates in-groups and out-groups and leaves rural students feeling unwelcome and unwanted in higher education. Materials and conversations about higher education can often be complex and confusing for rural students.

Materials

This study requested informational, recruitment mailings from the two-year and four-year higher education institutions within the state. Only a small portion of the institutions sent the requested hard copy materials, which was both interesting and disturbing. If institutions are not responding to requests for information, then how are rural students supposed to learn more about colleges and universities, including the admissions and financial aid processes? It is important that admissions offices at colleges and universities pay more attention to the information requests of all students but particularly students from underrepresented populations, such as rural students. Students often request hard copy information because they have limited access to technology or need something tangible to review with their parents or families.

Additionally, the few materials that were sent all used varying amounts of university jargon terms and none of them explained the meaning of that jargon. This creates a situation where, even when rural students receive recruitment information from colleges and universities, it is not likely that they completely understand the information. If a rural student cannot decipher the admissions materials, they may question their college-readiness and aspirations. Admissions offices can reduce these issues by being more aware of the language and terminology they use in their recruitment materials and, if they choose to use jargon, provide definitions or explanations for terms that are not often common knowledge for rural students and other underrepresented student populations. In addition, admissions offices could consider developing different sets of materials for different populations in an effort to target market to rural students and utilize broader language.

Recruiter Visits

Although Ms. Guillory mentioned that she felt confident that recruiters would visit MapDot High School if they were asked, the only data in this study that showed higher education recruiter interest in the rural area was institutions' participation in the County Career Day once per year. Recruiters came to the area for a half-day to set up a table and have short conversations with a limited number of students, all of whom were either eleventh or twelfth graders. There does not seem to be any recruiter involvement with rural students during the earlier high school years, which research shows is the most crucial time for developing college aspirations (Choy, 2001; Hossler & Gallagher, 1987). Higher education institutions and their recruitment and admissions offices should direct their recruiters to devote more of their time to connecting with rural students, especially those in ninth and tenth grades (Ganss, 2016). This would give rural students access to college "experts" who may have more accurate information and would allow students to have more time to learn about and consider institutional types and higher education options.

THEORETICAL AND RESEARCH IMPLICATIONS

Theory and prior research grounded and guided this study, and the findings tend to support theory and prior research. Findings from this study relate to two theoretical concepts—Hossler and Gallagher's (1987) College Choice Model and Bourdieu's concepts of cultural capital and habitus. The findings also further explore Vargas' (2004) study for The Education Resources Institute (TERI); research on counselors from Bickel et al. (1991), McDonough et al. (2010), and Paulsen and Loflink (2005); and research on rural education from Corbett (2009), Flora et al. (1992), Kelly (2009), McDonough et al. (2010), and Thebold and Siskar (2008).

Hossler and Gallagher's College Choice Model: Stage One and Stage Two

Hossler and Gallagher's (1987) three-phase college choice model was used as a framework for the MapDot High School case study to analyze both "individual and organizational factors to produce college choice outcomes" (p. 208). Stage One and Stage Two of the model—students' predisposition (or aspirations) and search (or access and options)—aligned with the tenth-grade standing of the participants and the stories they shared about their experiences with college access (see chapter 3 for a review of the model). The rural students were discerning what value they, and their communities, placed on education; determining if their financial resources and academic abilities would allow them to pursue higher education; and seeking support and information from people around them. Individually, students' background characteristics—particularly the social class of their household, their academic aptitude, and their parents' and peers' attitudes and encouragement to pursue higher education—significantly shaped their predisposition (Hossler & Gallagher, 1987).

A few rural students were further along in the predisposition phase because the curricular and extracurricular activities in which they engaged—honors classes, sports, clubs—gave them access to a college campus and were the type of activities valued by colleges and universities, unlike some of their peers who preferred hobbies like hunting and fishing or gaming. However, the rurality of the area and limitations of school resources did constrain the overall availability of opportunities that students could pursue to gain attention from institutions of higher education, which connected to rural students' predispositions (Hossler & Gallagher, 1987). Only one or two of the eight rural students in the study seemed to have transitioned to the search phase of Hossler and Gallagher's (1987) model. These students typically possessed cultural capital from participation in school activities or had someone close to them who could serve as a role model and information source.

Overall, rural students seemed to be stunted in the predisposition phase based on their underdeveloped college knowledge and challenge with decoding university jargon. Many students did not know what questions to ask about college, nor did they understand that their knowledge about college and its choice process was delayed. Hossler and Gallagher (1987) point out that during the search phase, students "discover the questions they should be asking . . . the differences between public and private, high cost and low cost, residential and non-residential, research and teaching institutions" and "need accurate information about types of institution" (p. 219). The MapDot High School students have yet to discover such questions and, even if or when they do, much of the information they would seek is difficult for them to obtain. Students who are from poor and working-class families and who are first-generation college students tend to have "longer and less efficient" searches and seek more assistance from their high school counselors (Hossler & Gallagher, 1987, p. 214). This affirms that rural, public high school counselors—like Ms. Guillory—are a key resource for rural students who intend to pursue higher education.

It would be beneficial for rural students to begin the search phase of Hossler and Gallagher's college choice model before, or during, their tenth-grade year because research shows that is when most students make postsecondary decisions (Choy, 2001). Rural, public high school districts and individual schools may need to focus on assisting students in their development from the predisposition phase to the search phase; educators need to have intentional higher education conversations and meetings with students during their earlier high school years and provide resources to students about where they can begin searching for information. The search process—and its dependence on accurate information—is highly connected to the rural community, school, and individual cultural capital and habitus.

Bourdieu's Cultural Capital and Habitus

Everyone possesses cultural capital; however, only some individuals possess the kind that is valuable and useful in educational institutions, which tend to endorse to dominant white, middle- and upper-class culture (Schwalbe et al., 2000). This study used Bourdieu's (1977) concepts of cultural capital and habitus to explore students' familiarity with college knowledge and how they sought to understand and comprehend university jargon. Bourdieu (1965) named language and communication as the most active and elusive parts of a person's cultural heritage and background. Rural students do not often naturally inherit the cultural capital that is vital to pursing higher education opportunities (McDonough, 1997). Higher education institutions also favor linguistic and cultural competencies that can "other" rural students and create barriers for them; as such, jargon is often an aspect of college knowledge that many rural students have trouble deciphering (Bourdieu, 1977; Whiting, 1999).

Vargas (2004) suggests that, even though the college knowledge gap is severe, it is not impossible to overcome, and he proposes policies for college access that focus on ways to provide underserved students with the information and guidance they need—both early and often. The findings of the MapDot case study, unfortunately, highlight that rural students are not currently receiving that kind of guidance, neither early nor often. Remedies could include starting conversations and information-sharing about higher education with students in eighth grade—when MapDot High School's counselor had her first academic track meeting with students—and continuing the college knowledge development process throughout the rest of students' high school careers.

College Knowledge and University Jargon

In addition to building the body of empirical work on Bourdieu's (1977) theory of cultural capital, this case study adds to the existing literature on university jargon, college knowledge, and college access. The focus on a rural population provided a new angle from which to study first-generation college students and poor and working-class students. Additionally, the study's specific focus on university jargon and college knowledge—as a function of cultural capital—addressed a gap in the literature and emphasized the relationship between jargon, college knowledge, aspiration, and, ultimately, access.

The relationship between these concepts offers an explanation about why rural, working-class, first-generation students are known to have lower educational aspirations than their peers with similar academic qualifications (HERI, 2007). The findings of this study also illuminate two of the relationships mentioned in Vargas' (2004) report for TERI—1) college-preparatory information and guidance are major components in students realizing college aspirations, and 2) students typically underrepresented in higher education lack the natural possession of college knowledge because they are members of families with limited or no college experience and attend schools that provide only minimal college guidance.

College guidance is a central component of Vargas's (2004) TERI report; it can also be a contested topic among both state and federal legislatures. For example, in the state in which this study took place, legislators made two policy decisions—requirement of ACT testing for all public high school students and proposed elimination of the public high school counselor position (both mentioned earlier in this chapter)—that highlight how government and public education are extremely intertwined. These policy decisions made at the state-level often have deep impacts on the functioning of rural, public high schools and, thus, the experiences of rural counselors and students.

Research on Counselors

Rural, public high school counselors could address many of the college aspiration and access factors for rural students by educating them on the academic, financial, and social aspects of their college options and providing suggestions on how to make informed, rational decisions that could result in higher rates of college aspiration and access (Bickel at al., 1991; Paulsen & Loflink, 2005). This study found that while counselors do attempt to provide these services and information, they face the significant constraints of overload and short-staffing that only allow sporadic college counseling until students reach their eleventh- or twelfth-grade years, if resources even permit at that time (see chapter 6).

Scholars call for the hiring of additional counselors who can make a special effort to provide underrepresented students with the college knowledge they need to turn their educational aspirations into realities (Bickel et al., 1991; Paulsen & Loflink, 2005). However, politicians and state education boards do not seem to agree with—or are ignoring—these research findings. The state's changes to the State School Handbook for School Administrators showed disregard for counselors and the many services they provide and invited schools to outsource counseling, which is in direct opposition to what scholars believe, and the findings of this study highlight, could help rural students navigate college knowledge and university jargon—MORE counselors!

Despite counselors' promising positive influence, McDonough et al. (2010) point out that counselors tend to possess limited and, often, outdated college information and funnel students to institutions near the rural area or its adjacent areas. Findings of this study support McDonough et al.'s (2010) critique because the counselors were only well versed in institutions within a two-hour radius of MapDot High School and did not seem to have support from the school or district to conduct campus visits to other institutions or seek professional development that could foster learning about new institutions, majors, or career fields. If counselors are only as helpful as the information they possess, their partial knowledge may restrict students' knowledge and postsecondary options.

Research on Rural Education

Some scholars view rural education in terms of loss because, for those who wish to have social class mobility, leaving the community is a common way to seek out "better" opportunities (Corbett, 2009; Flora et al., 1992; Kelly, 2009; McDonough et al., 2010). Rural schools have often become a means of "saving talented youth and sending them on to urban places" where they will be offered what is seen as countless education and job opportunities (Thebold & Siskar, 2008, p. 294), which becomes an issue of "brain drain" (Corbett, 2007). In short, success in many rural communities involves leaving; however, leaving—particularly to pursue higher education—is often a major financial issue for rural students (Corbett, 2009).

The case study of MapDot questioned the concept of rural education as loss or leaving. Although the issue of "brain drain" did arise in conversations with students and when discussing a lack of role models in the community, students did not seem to believe they had to leave the community to become successful or obtain the "better life" they consistently referenced. Rather, they mostly spoke of educational aspirations at institutions in close proximity to their hometown that would allow them to either continue residing in the area or visit easily and frequently. With the exception of two participants, students did not seem to have a mentality of wanting out of MapDot nor did they express a desire for "city life." Staying close to home may also be a tactic to deal with financial issues; participants continuously referenced their concerns about paying for college and noted that attending an institution in close proximity could alleviate some financial concerns. Overall, the study did support Corbett's (2007) finding that the link between education and community departure is "for some students . . . liberating, for others unthinkable, and for most it is problematic and conflicted" (p. 18).

This study also supported Corbett's (2009) finding that inequitable access on the basis of place is a fundamental barrier for rural students' higher education participation. The rural location of a school is considered a dimension of unequal educational opportunity and students from rural schools often possess lower levels of educational aspiration, attendance, and choice (Hu, 2003). This study expands Hu's findings to show that students' location in a rural area also contributes to their lower levels of college knowledge, which further complicates their higher education aspirations, attendance, and choice. Further research on rural communities and their education systems would help add to the findings of this study and others (Corbett, 2009; Flora et al., 1992; Kelly, 2009; McDonough et al., 2010; Thebold & Siskar, 2008).

LIMITATIONS AND SUGGESTIONS FOR FUTURE RESEARCH

All research studies make necessary choices that limit the scope of the study and its transferability. This study's theoretical framework was limited to cultural capital because prior higher education research shows that cultural capital most often relates to college knowledge and rural sociology research acknowledges that rural schools and areas often lack this type of capital (Corbett, 2007; Chenoweth & Gallagher, 2004; Flora et al., 1992; McDonough et al., 2010; Vargas, 2004; Willis, 1977). For example, Jencks (1972) describes how cultural attitudes and values for schooling influence rural students' educational aspirations and attainment more than either aptitude or finances. However, it would benefit future scholars and researchers to expand the study of rural college access to explore other forms of capital including but not limited to financial, social, familial, linguistic, and resistant capitals (see Yosso's 2005 community cultural wealth model). It would also be interesting to conduct a similar study focusing solely on the issue of financial capital because social class and income seem to be significant barriers for rural students, which is showcased by rural students' knowledge and identification of financial jargon in comparison to other jargon types.

This case study also focused on eight sophomore students and two counselors within two public high schools in one rural county in the southeastern United States. This choice was based on research that suggests the tenth-grade year as the ideal time when postsecondary options are typically highly considered (Choy, 2001). The study's small sample may limit its transferability to other rural areas, schools, or students. It would be useful to replicate this study in other rural areas both within the same state and around the country to determine if the findings are widely applicable to all rural areas. It may also be beneficial to replicate the study with varying student groups. This study looked at a cross-section of working-class, first-generation, rural students in tenth-grade who represented the gender and racial demographics of their respective public high schools. It would be interesting to narrow students' identities to explore how students' classification in school (ninth, tenth, eleventh, or twelfth grades), gender, race, or social class status influenced their acquisition and command of college knowledge and university jargon. Future studies could expand the population scope to include participation of students' parents and families as a way to explore broader issues of capital, habitus, and college knowledge.

Finally, it may be interesting to study teachers' and administrators' college knowledge and university jargon. Students often turn to these individuals to assist in their awareness and understanding of college knowledge and university jargon, and it seemed that rural school personnel have limited information themselves. It would be helpful to discover what college knowledge local, district-, and state-level personnel could identify and define and if—or how—they saw themselves playing a part in students' college aspirations and access.

CONCLUSION

This qualitative case study on how rural students obtain and comprehend college knowledge and decode university jargon informs both the PK-12 and higher education systems on how they can better prepare both rural counselors and students to engage in college counseling and provides implications for theory, practice, and policy. It is apparent that rural students are not receiving college information as early as is suggested in college access literature and rural students, their public high school counselors, higher education institutions, and state policymakers are all responsible for narrowing the gap between rural students' acquisition and comprehension of college knowledge and university jargon.

It is also important to note that the issue of rural students' obtaining and comprehending college knowledge and university jargon is an enduring issue. As a rural, first-generation, working-class college student myself, I experienced my own struggle with seeking and understanding college knowledge and decoding university jargon, not only as an undergraduate student 17 years ago, but also as a graduate student and, now, as a faculty member. Both PK-12 and higher education need to assess their environments for systematic structural, cultural, and social stratification issues that could be—or, one could argue, are—creating systemic challenges for rural students in obtaining and comprehending college knowledge and university jargon.

It is important that higher education, rural sociology, and social justice researchers continue to research rural experiences. While this population does not receive a lot of attention from scholars, rural experiences should be studied from various lenses of identity including but not limited to social class and capital, gender, race, and family composition. Rural students and those who educate them are a unique, multifaceted population whose stories should be heard. Their experiences are real, varied, and valid, and rural students deserve to have equitable opportunities for learning and development—at every level of education.

Appendix A

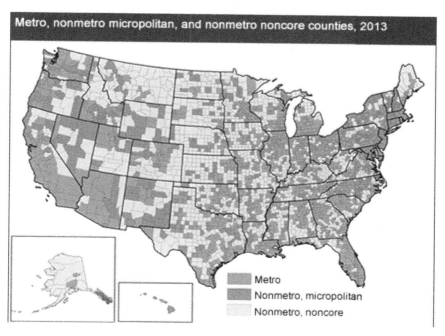

Figure A.1 United States Department of Agriculture Economic Research Service Nonmetropolitan Map.

Appendix B

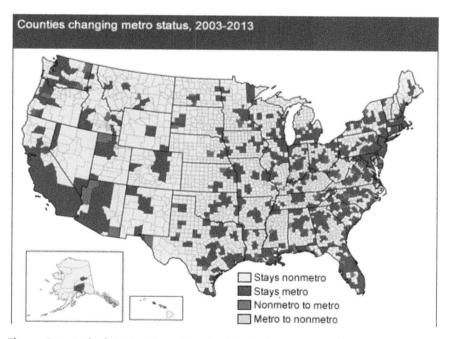

Figure B.1   United States Department of Agriculture Economic Research Service Changing Metro Status Map.

Appendix C

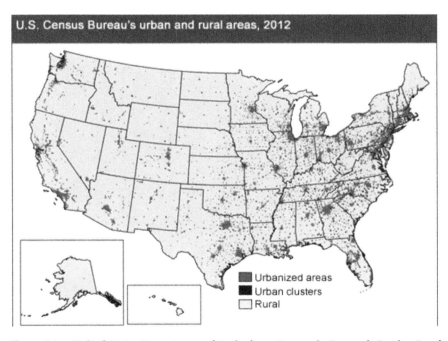

Figure C.1   United States Department of Agriculture Economic Research Service Rural Areas Map.

Appendix D

Table D.1   2015 Census Data for MapDot, USA

Population	
Population estimates, July 1, 2015, (V2015)	33,743
Population estimates base, April 1, 2010, (V2015)	33,984
Population, percent change—April 1, 2010 (estimates base) to July 1, 2015, (V2015)	-0.7%
Population, Census, April 1, 2010	33,984
Age and Sex	
Persons under 5 years, percent, July 1, 2015, (V2015)	6.9%
Persons under 5 years, percent, April 1, 2010	7.5%
Persons under 18 years, percent, July 1, 2015, (V2015)	25.8%
Persons under 18 years, percent, April 1, 2010	27.0%
Persons 65 years and over, percent, July 1, 2015, (V2015)	14.5%
Persons 65 years and over, percent, April 1, 2010	13.2%
Female persons, percent, July 1, 2015, (V2015)	48.9%
Female persons, percent, April 1, 2010	49.6%
Race and Hispanic Origin	
White alone, percent, July 1, 2015, (V2015) (a)	69.5%
White alone, percent, April 1, 2010 (a)	69.0%
Black or African American alone, percent, July 1, 2015, (V2015) (a)	28.6%
Black or African American alone, percent, April 1, 2010 (a)	28.3%
American Indian and Alaska Native alone, percent, July 1, 2015, (V2015) (a)	0.4%
American Indian and Alaska Native alone, percent, April 1, 2010 (a)	0.3%
Asian alone, percent, July 1, 2015, (V2015) (a)	0.4%
Asian alone, percent, April 1, 2010 (a)	0.3%
Native Hawaiian and Other Pacific Islander alone, percent, July 1, 2015, (V2015) (a)	Z
Native Hawaiian and Other Pacific Islander alone, percent, April 1, 2010 (a)	Z
Two or More Races, percent, July 1, 2015, (V2015)	1.1%
Two or More Races, percent, April 1, 2010	1.1%

(Continued)

Table D.1   2015 Census Data for MapDot, USA (Continued)

Hispanic or Latino, percent, July 1, 2015, (V2015) (b)	3.2%
Hispanic or Latino, percent, April 1, 2010 (b)	2.3%
White alone, not Hispanic or Latino, percent, July 1, 2015, (V2015)	67.2%
White alone, not Hispanic or Latino, percent, April 1, 2010	67.9%

Population Characteristics

Veterans, 2010–2014	1,886
Foreign born persons, percent, 2010–2014	1.9%

Housing

Housing units, July 1, 2015, (V2015)	14,909
Housing units, April 1, 2010	14,662
Owner-occupied housing unit rate, 2010–2014	66.0%
Median value of owner-occupied housing units, 2010-2014	$79,800
Median selected monthly owner costs -with a mortgage, 2010–2014	$857
Median selected monthly owner costs -without a mortgage, 2010–2014	$300
Median gross rent, 2010–2014	$514
Building permits, 2015	47

Families and Living Arrangements

Households, 2010–2014	12,053
Persons per household, 2010–2014	2.62
Living in same house 1 year ago, percent of persons age 1 year+, 2010–2014	88.6%
Language other than English spoken at home, percent of persons age 5 years+, 2010–2014	19.7%

Education

High school graduate or higher, percent of persons age 25 years+, 2010–2014	68.2%
Bachelor's degree or higher, percent of persons age 25 years+, 2010–2014	12.6%

Health

With a disability, under age 65 years, percent, 2010–2014	15.9%
Persons without health insurance, under age 65 years, percent	16.6%

Economy

In civilian labor force, total, percent of population age 16 years+, 2010–2014	47.7%
In civilian labor force, female, percent of population age 16 years+, 2010–2014	45.9%
Total accommodation and food services sales, 2012 ($1,000) (c)	D
Total health care and social assistance receipts/revenue, 2012 ($1,000) (c)	184,311
Total manufacturers shipments, 2012 ($1,000) (c)	D
Total merchant wholesaler sales, 2012 ($1,000) (c)	72,180
Total retail sales, 2012 ($1,000) (c)	213,742
Total retail sales per capita, 2012 (c)	$6,341

Transportation

Mean travel time to work (minutes), workers age 16 years+, 2010–2014	30.4

Income and Poverty

Median household income (in 2014 dollars), 2010–2014	$30,323
Per capita income in past 12 months (in 2014 dollars), 2010–2014	$18,535
Persons in poverty, percent	24.1%

BUSINESSES

Total employer establishments, 2014	528
Total employment, 2014	6,505
Total annual payroll, 2014	193,351
Total employment, percent change, 2013–2014	-0.2%
Total nonemployer establishments, 2014	1,578
All firms, 2012	2,152
Men-owned firms, 2012	1,198
Women-owned firms, 2012	642
Minority-owned firms, 2012	460
Nonminority-owned firms, 2012	1,603
Veteran-owned firms, 2012	209
Nonveteran-owned firms, 2012	1,823

GEOGRAPHY

Population per square mile, 2010	51.3
Land area in square miles, 2010	662.38

Appendix E

Low education counties, 2015 edition

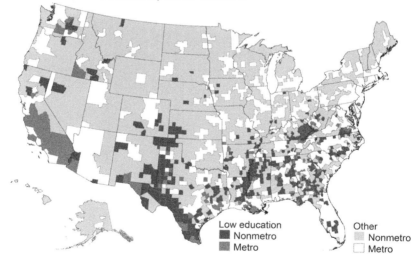

Low education counties are those where 20 percent or more of county residents age 25-64 did not have a high school diploma or equivalent, determined by the American Community Survey 5-year average data for 2008-12.
Note that county boundaries are drawn for the low education counties only.
Source: USDA, Economic Research Service using data from U.S. Census Bureau.

Figure E.1   United States Department of Agriculture Economic Research Service Low-Education Counties Map.

Appendix F

Persistent poverty counties, 2015 edition

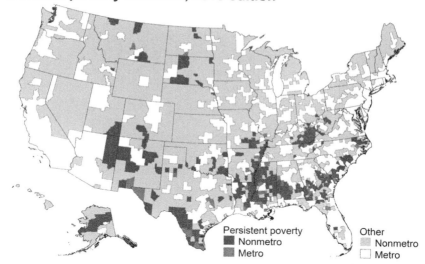

Persistent poverty counties are those where 20 percent or more of county residents were poor, measured by the 1980, 1990, 2000 censuses, and the 2007-11 American Community Survey.
Note that county boundaries are drawn for the persistent poverty counties only.
Source: USDA, Economic Research Service using data from U.S. Census Bureau.

Figure F.1 United States Department of Agriculture Economic Research Service Persistent Poverty Counties Map.

Appendix G

This list is a compilation of terms used in university admissions and financial aid documents, course catalogs, and viewbooks. These terms/acronyms are not necessarily known by people prior to going to college.

Table G.1   College and University Jargon/Terms

General Terms	Academic Terms	Financial Terms	Degree Terms
1. Community College	14. ACT/SAT	36. FAFSA	47. A.A.
2. Junior College	15. AP	37. Tuition (in-state and out-of-state)	48. A.S.
3. Technical College	16. IB	38. Fees	49. A.A.S.
4. College	17. Accredited	39. Room and Board	50. B.A.
5. University (with Colleges and/or Schools)	18. Full-Time	40. Scholarships	51. B.S.
6. Public (and/or Land-Grant)	19. Part-Time	41. Grants	52. Master's
7. Private	20. Credit Hours	42. Subsidized Loans	53. Doctoral
8. PWI	21. Major	43. Unsubsidized Loans	54. Professional (Law, Medical, etc.)
9. HBCU	22. Minor	44. Work Study	
10. HSI	23. Specialization	45. TOPS	
11. AANAPI	24. Certificate	46. TRIO/Transition Programs	
12. Faculty Staff	25. Liberal Arts		
13. Alumni	26. General Education Requirements		
	27. Degree Audit		
	28. Degree Requirements		
	29. Prerequisite		
	30. Section		
	31. Drop/Add		
	32. Open/Closed/Waitlist		
	33. Syllabus		
	34. Semester		
	35. Quarter		

References

Advocate Editorial. (2016, September 7). Our view: Progress, point by point on the ACT test. *The Advocate*. Retrieved from http://www.theadvocate.com/baton_rouge/opinion/article_aafbb90a-6ef3–11e6-bc9c-dfca2ada239f.html

Archer, L. (2003a). Social class and higher education. In L. Archer, M. Hutchings, & A. Ross (Eds.), *Higher education and social class: Issues of exclusion and inclusion*. New York: RoutledgeFalmer.

Archer, L. (2003b). The 'value' of higher education. In L. Archer, M. Hutchings, & A. Ross (Eds.), *Higher education and social class: Issues of exclusion and inclusion*. New York: RoutledgeFalmer.

Archer, L., Hutchings, M., & Ross, A. (2003). *Higher education and social class: Issues of exclusion and inclusion*. New York: RoutledgeFalmer.

Aronson, P. (2008). Breaking barriers or locked out? Class-based perceptions and experiences of postsecondary education. *New Directions for Child Adolescent Development,* 119, 41–54.

Barratt, W. (2011). *Social class on campus: Theories and manifestations*. Sterling, VA: Stylus Publishing.

Baum, S., Ma, J., & Payea, K. (2010). *Education pays 2010*. Washington, DC: College Board. Retrieved from http://trends.collegebound.org/downloads/Education_Pays_2010.pdf

Bell, A. D., Rowan-Kenyon, H., & Perna, L. W. (2009). College knowledge of 9th and 11th grade students: Variation by school and state context. *Journal of Higher Education,* 80(6), 663–685. Retrieved from http://search.ebscohost.com/login.aspx?direct=true&db=eric&AN=EJ861124&site=ehost-live&scope=site; http://www.ohiostatepress.org/Journals/JHE/jhemain.htm

Bergerson, A. A., Heiselt, A. K., & Aiken-Wisniewski, S. (2013). Refocusing college choice: Women's reflections on their postsecondary education choices. *NASPA Journal About Women in Higher Education,* 6(2), 185–211.

Bickel, R., Banks, S., & Spatig, L. (1991). Bridging the gap between high school and college in an Appalachian state: A near-replication of Florida research. *Journal of Research in Rural Education,* 7(2), 75–87.

Bourdieu, P., Passeron, J. C., & de Saint Martin, M. (1965). *Academic discourse: Linguistic misunderstanding and professorial power.* Stanford, CA: Stanford University Press.

Bourdieu, P. (1977). *Reproduction in education, society, and culture.* London: Sage Publishing.

Bourdieu, P. (1984). *Distinction: A social critique of the judgment of taste.* Cambridge, MA: Harvard University Press.

Bourdieu, P. (1986). The forms of capital. In J. Richardson (Ed.), *Handbook of theory and research for the sociology of education.* New York: Greenwood.

Brown, D. & Swanson, L. (2003). *Challe nges for rural America in the twenty-first century.* University Park, PA: Pennsylvania State University Press.

Bruni, F. (2015). *Where you go is not who you'll be: An antidote to the college admissions mania.* New York: Grand Central Publishing.

Bruni, F. (2016, September 17). Why college rankings are a joke. *The New York Times.* Retrieved from http://www.nytimes.com/2016/09/18/opinion/sunday/why-college-rankings-are-a-joke.html?_r=0

Byun, S., Irvin, M. J., & Meece, J. L. (2012). Predictors of bachelor's degree completion among rural students at four-year institutions. *The Review of Higher Education,* 35(3), 463–484.

Cabrera, A. F., & LaNasa, S. M. (2001). On the path to college: Three critical tasks facing American's disadvantaged. *Research in Higher Education,* 42(2), 119–150.

Carr, P. J. & Kefalas, M. (2009). *Hollowing out the middle: The rural brain drain and what it means for America.* Boston, MA: Beacon Press.

Chenoweth, E., & Galliher, R. (2004). Factors influencing college aspirations of rural West Virginia high school students. *Journal of Research in Rural Education,* 19(2), 1–14.

Choy, S. P. (2001). *Students whose parents did not go to college: Postsecondary access, persistence, and attainment* (NCES 2001–126). Washington, DC: U.S. Department of Education National Center for Education Statistics. Retrieved from http://nces.ed.gov/pubs2001/2001126.pdf

Conley, D. T. (2005). *College knowledge: What it really takes for students to succeed and what we can do to get them ready.* San Francisco: Jossey-Bass.

Corbett, M. (2007). *Learning to leave: The irony of schooling in a coastal community.* Black Point, Nova Scotia, Canada: Fernwood Publishing.

Corbett, M. (2009). Rural schooling in mobile modernity: Returning to the places I've been. *Journal of Research in Rural Education,* 24(7), 1–13.

County School Board. (2010). *Graduation cohort rates report.* Retrieved from http://www.epsb.com

Creswell, J. (2007). *Qualitative inquiry & research design: Choosing among five approaches.* Thousand Oaks, CA: Sage.

Cushman, K. (2007). Facing the culture shock of college. *Educational Leadership,* 64(7), 44–47.

Dumais, S. A. & Ward, A. (2009). Cultural capital and first-generation college success. *Poetics,* 38(3), 245–265.

Flora, C. B., Flora, J. L., & Gasteyer, S. P. (2016). *Rural communities: Legacy & change* (5th ed.). Boulder, CO: Westview Press.

Flora, C. B., Flora, J. L., Spears, J. D., & Swanson, L. E. (1992). *Rural communities: Legacy & change.* Boulder, CO: Westview Press.

Ganss, K. M. (2016). The college transition for first-year students from rural Oregoncommunities. *Journal of Student Affairs Research and Practice,* 53(3), 269–280.

Gee, J. (1998). What is literacy? In V. Zamel & R. Spack (Eds.), *Negotiating academic literacies: Teaching and learning across languages and cultures.* Mahwah, NJ: Lawrence Erlbaum Associates, Publishers.

Gentzel, T. J. (2012, April 25). ACT college entrance exams to be required for all high school juniors. *The Huffington Post.* Retrieved from http://www.huffingtonpost.com/2012/04/25/act-college-entrance-exam_n_1452992.html.

Goldrick-Rab, S. (2016). *Paying the price: College costs, financial aid, and the betrayal of the American dream.* Chicago, IL: The University of Chicago Press.

Griffin, D., Hutchins, B. C., & Meece, J. L. (2011). Where do rural students go to find information about their futures? *Journal of Counseling and Development,* 89(2), 172–181.

Harris, E. (2014, December 25). Little college guidance: 500 high school students per counselor. *The New York Times.* Retrieved from http://www.nytimes.com/2014/12/26/nyregion/little-college-guidance-500-high-school-students-per-counselor.html

Hearn, J. C., Phones, A. P., & Kurban, E. R. (2013). Access, persistence, and completion in the state context. In L. Perna & A. P. Jones (Eds.), *The state of college access and completion: Improving college success for student from underrepresented groups.* New York: Routledge.

Heller, D. (2013). The role of finances in postsecondary access and success. In L. Perna & A. P. Jones (Eds.), *The state of college access and completion: Improving college success for student from underrepresented groups.* New York: Routledge.

Hesse-Biber, S. & Leavy, P. (2011). *The practice of qualitative research.* Thousand Oaks, CA: Sage.

Higher Education Research Institute Research Brief. (2007). *First in my family: A profile of first-generation college students at four-year institutions since 1971.* Los Angeles, CA: Higher Education Research Institute, University of California, Los Angeles.

Hossler, D. & Gallagher, K. (1987). Studying student college choice: A three-phase model and the implications for policymakers. *College and University,* 62, 207–221.

Hossler, D. & Palmer, M. (2012). Why understand research on college choice? In National Association for College Admission Counsel (Eds.), *Fundamentals of college admissions counseling: A textbook for graduate students and practicing counselors.* Dubuque, IA: Kendall Hunt Publishing.

Howley, C. B. & Howley, A. (2010). Poverty and school achievement in rural communities: A social-class interpretation. In K. A. Schafft & A. Y. Jackson (Eds.), *Rural education for the twenty-first century: Identity, place, and community in a globalizing world.* University Park, PA: The Pennsylvania State University Press.

Hu, S. (2003). Educational aspirations and postsecondary access and choice: Students in urban, suburban, and rural schools compared. *Education Policy Analysis Archives,* 11(14), 1–13.

Hurst, A. L. (2012). *College and the working class: What it takes to make it.* Rotterdam, The Netherlands: Sense Publishers.

Isserman, A. (2005). In the national interest: Defining rural and urban correctly in research and public policy. *International Regional Science Review, 28*(4), 465–499.

James, R., Wyn, J., Baldwin, G., Hepwroth, G., McInnis, C., & Stephanou, A. (1999). *Rural and isolated school students and their higher education choices: A reexamination of student location, socioeconomic background, and educational advantage and disadvantage.* Australia: National Board of Employment, Education and Training: Higher Education Council.

Jencks, C. (1972). *Inequality: A reassessment of the effect of family and schooling in America.* New York: Basic Books.

Johnson, J., Showalter, D., Klein, R., & Lester, C. (2014). *Why rural matters 2013–2014: The condition of rural education in the 50 states.* Washington, DC: The Rural School and Community Trust. Retrieved from http://www.ruraledu.org/user_uploads/file/2013–14-Why-Rural-Matters.pdf

Johnson, J. & Strange, M. (2005). *Why rural matters 2005.* Washington, DC: Rural School and Community Trust. Retrieved from http://files.ruraledu.org/whyrural-matters/ WRM2005.pdf

Jones, A. P. (2013). Introduction. Improving postsecondary access, persistence, and completion in the United States: Setting the stage. In L. Perna & A. P. Jones (Eds.), *The state of college access and completion: Improving college success for student from underrepresented groups.* New York: Routledge.

Kamenetz, A. (2016, September 16). *New college rankings are out! NPR Ed rates the rankings!* Retrieved from http://www.npr.org/sections/ed/2016/09/13/493144907/new-college-rankings-are-out-npr-ed-rates-the-rankings

Kelly, U. (2009). Learning to lose: Rurality, transience, and belonging (a companion to Michael Corbett). *Journal of Research in Rural Education, 24*(11).

Kempner, K. (1991). Understanding cultural conflict. In W. G. Tierney (Ed.), *Culture and ideology in Higher Education: Advancing a critical agenda.* New York: Praeger.

Kim, S. & Kim, H. (2009). Does cultural capital matter? Cultural divide and quality of life. *Social Indicators Research, 93*(2), 295–319.

Krathwohl, D. R. (2009). *Methods of educational and social science research: An integrated approach* (3rd ed.). Long Grove, IL: Waveland Press.

Kusmin, L. D. (2011). *Rural America at a glance (Economic Information Bulletin No. 85).* Washington, DC: United States Department of Agriculture, Economic Research Service. Retrieved from http://www.ers.usda.gov/publications/eib-economic-information-bulletin/eib85.aspx#.U1HAKhCRItU

MacLeod, J. (2009). *Ain't no makin' it: Aspirations and attainment in a low-income neighborhood.* Philadelphia, PA: Westview Press.

Mantsios, G. (2013). Class in America—2006. In M. Adams, W. Blumenfeld, C. R. Castaneda, H. W. Hackman, M. L. Peters, & X. Zuniga (Eds.), *Readings for diversity and social justice* (3rd ed.) (pp. 150–156). New York: Rutledge.

Martin, G. L. (2015). "Always in my face": An exploration of social class consciousness, salience, & values. *Journal of College Student Development, 56*(5), 471–487.

McDonough, P. M. (1997). *Choosing colleges: How social class and schools structure opportunity.* Albany: SUNY Press.

McDonough, P. M., Gildersleeve, R. E., & Jarsky, K. M. (2010). The golden cage of rural college access: How higher education can respond to the rural life. In Schafft & Jackson (Eds.), *Rural education for the twenty-first century: Identity, place, and community in a globalizing world* (pp. 191–209). University Park, PA: Pennsylvania University Press.

McGill, K. (2015, August 27). [State] improves ACT test scores but still ranks below national average. *The Advocate.* Retrieved from http://www.theadvocate.com/baton_rouge/news/education/article_f4dc9baf-a596–5199–99a3–599d6d59cac8.html

Merriam, S. (2009). *Qualitative research: A guide to design and implementation.* San Francisco: Jossey-Bass.

Mertens, D. M. (2010). *Research and evaluation in education and psychology: Integrating diversity with quantitative, qualitative, and mixed methods* (3rd ed.). Thousand Oaks, CA: Sage.

Mullen, A. L. (2010). *Degrees of inequality: Culture, class, and gender in American higher education.* Baltimore, MD: The John Hopkins University Press.

National Center for Education Statistics. (2006). *Status of education in rural America.* Washington, DC: Author. Retrieved January 19, 2012, from http://nces.ed.gov/pubs2007/2007040.pdf

National Center for Educational Statistics. (2011). *Percentage of persons ages 18–29 enrolled in colleges or universities, by age group, locale, and sex: 2011.* [Table B.3.b.-1]. Retrieved from http://nces.ed.gov/surveys/ruraled/tables_archive.asp

National Center for Educational Statistics. (2013). *The status of rural education (spotlight).* Washington, DC: Institute of Education Sciences, U.S. Department of Education. Retrieved from http://nces.ed.gov/programs/coe/indicator_tla.asp

National College Access Network Member Directory. (2010). Retrieved November 19, 2010, from http://www.collegeaccess.org/member_directory.aspx#New%20Hamp

O'Quinn, M. (1999). Getting above our raising: A case study of women from the coalfields of Southwest Virginia and Eastern Kentucky. *Journal of Research in Rural Education,* 15(3), 181–189.

Pappano, L. (2017, January 31). Colleges discover the rural student. *The New York Times.* Retrieved from https://www.nytimes.com/2017/01/31/education/edlife/colleges-discover-rural-student.html?mcubz=0

Patton, M. (2002). *Qualitative research and evaluation methods.* Thousand Oaks, CA: Sage.

Paulsen, M. B. (2001). The economics of human capital and investment in higher education. In M. B. Paulsen & J. C. Smart (Eds.). *The finance of higher education: Theory, research policy, and practice.* New York: Agathon.

Paulsen, M. & Lohfink, M. (2005). Comparing the determinants of persistence for first-generation and continuing-generation students. *Journal of College Student Development,* 46(4), 409–428.

Perna, L. (2013). Improving college access, persistence, and completion: Lessons learned. In L. Perna & A. P. Jones (Eds.), *The state of college access and completion: Improving college success for student from underrepresented groups.* New York: Routledge.

Perna, L. & Kurban, E. R. (2013). Improving college access and choice. In L. Perna & A. P. Jones (Eds.), *The state of college access and completion: Improving college success for student from underrepresented groups.* New York: Routledge.

Porterfield, D. (2017, April 20). We can't afford not to launch rural youth into college success. *The Hechinger Report.* Retrieved from http://hechingerreport.org/opinion-cant-afford-not-launch-rural-youth-college-success/

Rosales, J. (2015, February 1). With new roles, school counselors are more indispensable than ever. *National Education Association Today.* Retrieved from http://neatoday.org/2015/02/01/school-counselors-are-more-indispensable-than-ever/

Sacks, P. (2007). *Tearing down the gates: Confronting the class divide in American education.* Berkeley, CA: University of California Press.

Schaft, K. & Jackson, A. Y. (2010). *Rural education for the twenty-first century: Identity, place, and community in a globalizing world.* University Park, PA: Pennsylvania University Press.

Scherer, J. L. & Anson, M. L. (2014). *Community colleges and the access effect: Why open admissions suppresses achievement.* New York: Palgrave Macmillan.

Schwalbe, M., Godwin, S., Holden, D., Schrock, D., Thompson, S., & Wolkomir, M. (2000). Generic processes in the reproduction of inequality: An interactionist analysis. *Social Forces, 79*(2), 419–452.

Sentell, W. (2016, July 25). State's ACT scores up slightly; more students qualify for college. *The Advocate.* Retrieved from http://www.theadvocate.com/baton_rouge/news/education/article_bb36bfe4–52ac-11e6-b529–7b70f6e4b85f.html

Sentell, W. (2012, November, 15). Students face tougher assessments. *The Advocate.* Retrieved from http://www.theadvocate.com/baton_rouge/news/education/article_cbf95b9d-a48e-5364–84ec-b606d42a1a7a.html

Sentell, W. (2013, January 16). BESE panel votes to revamp role of school counselors. *The Advocate.* Retrieved from http://www.theadvocate.com/baton_rouge/news/education/article_1f39f486-bc88–5b46-bca4-eebe96a7e160.html

Simmons, L., & Bryan, E. (2009). Family involvement: Impacts on post-secondary educational success for first-generation Appalachian college students. *Journal of College Student Development, 50*(4), 391–406.

Soria, K. M. (2015). *Welcoming blue-collar scholars into the ivory tower: Developing class-consciousness strategies for student success.* Columbia, SC: University of South Carolina, National Resource Center for the First-Year Experience and Students in Transition.

Stake, R. (1995). *The art of case study research.* Thousand Oaks, CA: Sage.

State Department of Administration—DOA. (2012). *Bulletin 741—[State] School Handbook for School Administrators.* Retrieved from http://www.doa.louisiana.gov/osr/lac/28v115/28v115.doc

State Department of Education. (2011a). *2011 District Rankings.* Retrieved from http://www.louisianaschools.net/data/district_accountability_reports.aspx

State Department of Education. (2011b). *Public School Student Enrollment Data (Multiple Statistics).* Retrieved from http://www.louisianaschools.net/offices/info-management/student_enrollment_data.html

State Department of Education. (2012). *Graduation Requirements.* Retrieved from http://www.louisianaschools.net/topics/grad_reqs.html#tab_1

Stuber, J. M. (2011). *Inside the college gates: How class and culture matter in higher education.* Lanham, MD: Rowman & Littlefield.

Theobald, P. & Siskar, J. (2008). Rural education. In T. Good (Ed.), *21st century education: A reference handbook* (pp. 292–299). Thousand Oaks, CA: Sage.

Tieken, M. C. (2014). *Why rural schools matter.* Chapel Hill, NC: The University of North Carolina Press.

Tramonte, L. & Willms, J. D. (2010). Cultural capital and its effects on education outcomes. *Economics of Education Review, 29*(2), 200–213.

United States Census Data. (2000). *Fact Sheet.* Retrieved November 10, 2010, from http://factfinder.census.gov

United States Census Data. (2010). *QuickFacts Sheet.* Retrieved from http://factfinder.census.gov

United States Census Data. (2010). *FactFinder Sheet.* Retrieved from http://factfinder.census.gov

United States Census Data. (2015). *QuickFacts Sheet.* Retrieved from http://factfinder.census.gov

United States Department of Agriculture Economic Research Service. (2003). *Rural education at a glance.* (USDA ERS Rural Development Research Report No. 98). Washington, DC: Author.

United States Department of Agriculture Economic Research Service. (2007). *Measuring rurality: What is rural?* Retrieved January 19, 2012, from http://www.ers.usda.gov/Briefing/Rurality/WhatIsRural

United States Department of Agriculture Economic Research Service. (2016). *Rural America at a glance.* (USDA ERS Economic Information Bulletin No. 162). Washington, DC: Author.

United States Department of Education, Institute of Education Sciences. (2007). *How the government defines rural has implications for education policies and practices.* (US DOE IES Issues & Answers REL 2007- No. 010). Washington, DC: Author.

United States Department of Education, National Center for Education Statistics. (2013). *The status of rural education.* (US DOE NCES Common Core of Data). Washington, DC: Author.

Vargas, J. (2004). *College knowledge: Addressing information barriers to college.* Boston, MA: Education Resources Institute.

Walpole, M. (2003). Socioeconomic status and college: How SES affects college experiences and outcomes. *Review of Higher Education, 27*(1), 45–73.

Warnock, D. M. (2016). Capitalizing class: An examination of socioeconomic diversity on the contemporary campus. In A. L. Hurst & S. K. Nenga (Eds.), *Working in class: Recognizing how social class shapes our academic work.* Lanham, MD: Rowman & Littlefield.

Wettersten, K. B., Guilmino, A., Herrick, C. G., Hunter, P. J., Kim, G. Y., Jagow, D., Beecher, T., Faul, K., Baker, A. A., Rudolph, S. E., Ellenbecker, K., & McCormick, J. (2005). Predicting educational and vocational attitudes among rural high school students. *Journal of Counseling Psychology, 52*(4), 658–663.

White, J. W. (2005). Sociolinguistic challenges to minority collegiate success: Entering the discourse community of the college. *Journal of College Student Retention: Research, Theory & Practice, 6*(4), 369–393.

Whiting, M. E. (1999). The university and the white, rural male. *Journal of Research in Rural Education, 15*(3), 157–164.

Willis, P. (1977). *Learning to labor: How working class kids get working class jobs.* New York, NY: Columbia University Press.

Yin, R. (2009). *Case study research: Design and methods.* Thousand Oaks, CA: Sage.

Yosso, T. (2005). Whose culture has capital? A critical race theory discussion of community cultural wealth. *Race, Ethnicity, and Education 8*(1), 69–91.

Zwerling, L. S. & London, H. B. (1992). First-generation students: Confronting the cultural issues. *New Directions for Community Colleges*, No.80. Los Angeles, CA: ERIC Clearinghouse for Junior Colleges.

Index

About the Author

Dr. Sonja Ardoin is an author, learner, educator, and facilitator. She originates from "Cajun country" and is proud of her first generation to PhD educational journey, including degrees from Louisiana State University, Florida State University, and North Carolina State University. Sonja's career path includes experience in student activities, leadership development, community engagement, fraternity and sorority life, student conduct, and academic advising. She is currently serving as program director and clinical assistant professor of higher education at Boston University. Sonja stays engaged in the field through presenting, facilitating, and volunteering with national organizations such as ASHE, NASPA, ACPA, LeaderShape, Zeta Tau Alpha, Lambda Chi Alpha, Delta Gamma, and College Summit. She authored *The Strategic Guide to Shaping Your Student Affairs Career* (2014), is engaged in multiple writing and research projects, and has consulted and given keynote addresses at a number of campuses across the United States. Sonja grew up poor and working class and still identifies as blue collar in many ways. She now studies the experiences of first-generation and rural students; poor and working-class students, faculty, and staff in higher education; student and women's leadership; and career pathways in student affairs. Sonja enjoys traveling, dancing, reading, writing, sports, laughing, and spending time with people she loves.